Y0-BBY-141

979.4
Da

C.1
7

Dawson, Grace S.
California.

DATE DUE			
1-4-65 208			
	208 white-parent		
NOV 11 '68	202	202	APR 80
DEC 2 '68			
MAR 25 1969			
NOV 30 1970 211			
Schnabel			
Hansen			

BERKELEY UNIFIED SCHOOL
DISTRICT LIBRARIES
Berkeley, California

OFFICIALLY WITHDRAWN

CALIFORNIA

The Story of Our Southwest Corner

A Manila Galleon

CALIFORNIA

THE STORY OF
Our Southwest Corner

By GRACE S. DAWSON

Illustrated by

LOREN BARTON

NEW YORK

THE MACMILLAN COMPANY

1962

LONGFELLOW SCHOOL LIBRARY
BERKELEY, CALIF.

COPYRIGHT, 1939, BY

GRACE S. DAWSON

All rights reserved—no part of this book may be reproduced in any form without permission in writing from the publisher, except by a reviewer who wishes to quote brief passages in connection with a review written for inclusion in magazine or newspaper.

———

Set up and electrotyped. Published April, 1939.
Sixteenth Printing, 1962

— PRINTED IN THE UNITED STATES OF AMERICA —

TO

R. E. D.

whose enthusiasm for the history of our great West began many years ago and followed the Santa Fe Trail to California, this book is dedicated.

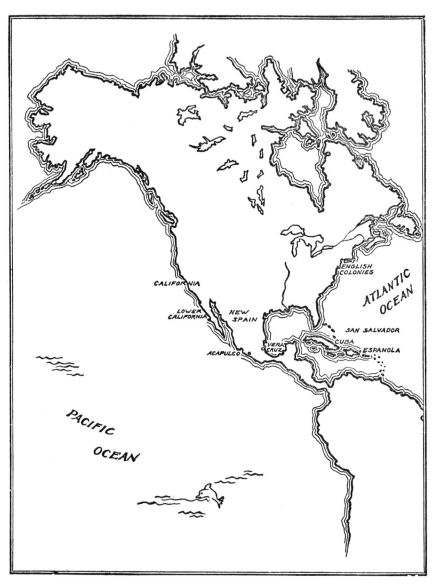

New World Colonies

✛✛

In the Southwest Corner

MOST OF the stories of our country begin with the east coast. This was the front gate of America. To this front gate, across the great highway of the Atlantic Ocean, came ships from England, Holland, and France. In the front yard of America, England and France fought for control of the new continent. England won. Then arose a new nation demanding freedom from the rule of England. This new nation, the United States, built the house of a strong and lasting government in the front yard of America.

Meanwhile the back yard of America stretched away for thousands of miles to the shore of the Pacific Ocean, an unknown shore of an unknown ocean. But Spain had built herself a house in the New World, next door to this back yard, in the country called Mexico. The Spanish heard wonderful tales about this unknown shore, tales of golden cities and islands of pearls. So they came searching for adventure and riches into the Southwest Corner of America's back yard.

They settled the wilderness. They conquered the natives. They brought with them their religion and their culture. They showed the world the beauty and promise of this new land, which they called California. They held it safely in spite of the envy of Russia, England, and France. But the power of Spain waned. Mexico threw off the rule of Spain and became an independent nation. And Mexico was not strong enough to hold California. The United States awoke to the value of this western coast, and claimed it for her own.

Then swift changes came to California, the back yard of America. The long expanse of hills and valleys, deserts and mountains, was turned into a fertile garden. It became a playground, too, a place of new and startling beauty. It was found to be a gateway facing another highway, the Pacific Ocean. The back yard became as important as the front yard.

These things belong to our country's past. They belong to us all. They need to be told along with the rest of the story of our country's growth. This is a story of our country which does not begin at the front gate. It begins in the Southwest Corner.

CONTENTS

CONTENTS

The Gold Rush

How California Grew

As the Spanish Say It

+++

SPANISH IS a beautiful and musical language. You will enjoy the story of California more if you know how to pronounce the many Spanish names of people and places as the Spanish do. Sometimes, too, you will need to find out what a name means.

Whenever you come to a name you do not know, turn to pages 205 to 206 at the back of the book and learn to pronounce it correctly. Suppose the new name is *Mission San Juan Bautista*. You will have three words to look up. Here they are:

San (Sahn), Saint

Juan (Hwan), John

Bautista (Bow-tees-ta), the Baptist

When you have looked up the three words you will know how to pronounce them, and you will know that *Mission San Juan Bautista* means *The Mission of Saint John the Baptist*.

The author takes pleasure in expressing her thanks and appreciation for kindly interest and assistance during the writing of this book to Dr. Robert Glass Cleland, Dean of Occidental College and distinguished historian; to Dr. Frederick Webb Hodge, Director of the Southwest Museum; and to Mr. Lindley Bynum, Field Representative of the Henry E. Huntington Library.

Thanks are due, also, to members of the staff of the Pasadena Public Library for untiring patience in small matters of research, and to the Macmillan Company for able and intelligent editorial assistance in preparing the manuscript for young readers.

Before the White Men Came

✠✠

CHAPTER I

The Indians of California

THE LAND we call California did not have that name before white men came to the new world. If it had a name at all it was an Indian name. For California was a land of Indians.

It was a beautiful land. High mountains towered over it, mountains whose tops were covered with snow all the year round. Forests covered their slopes. At their feet were lovely valleys, which were sometimes green, sometimes brown, and sometimes blue or purple or gold with blooming flowers. Noisy streams rushed and dashed between the high gray boulders of canyons.

West of the mountains was a long shore line, where ocean waves came rolling up the beach or foamed among the rocks. Beyond the mountains to the east were vast desert places. Here strange plants grew, and white sands reflected the hot sun at noon and the round white moon at night.

This land was not only beautiful, it was also rich. Hidden in the rocks of the mountains was gold. Under the rolling plains and hills was oil. The soil was rich enough, under the warm sunshine, to produce oranges and grapes and many other delicious fruits and vegetables. The air was like magic. It was so light and dry and full of sunshine that it could make sick people well and make well people stronger and healthier.

Any nation would have been glad to possess such a land as this was, had the nations of that time known about it. But they did not know. Even the Indians who lived there did not know how wonderful their country was.

There were many thousands of these Indians. Some of them were dark-skinned, almost black; others were brown-skinned; still others were no darker than a light tan. Some were very large and strong; others were short. They varied in languages as well as in looks. Many different tongues were spoken and more than one hundred different dialects. The Indians of one group could not understand the Indians of the others. Their ways of living differed also. Those who lived in the mountains built different kinds of houses and ate different kinds of food from those who lived in the river valleys or close to the seashore.

It would take a whole book to tell how each of the different tribes lived. So we will divide them into three classes: the Northern, the Southern, and the Central Indians.

Let us go back to that faraway time and visit the home of an Indian family in each of these sections. This will give us some idea of how they lived.

In the most northern part of California the mountains were

near the sea. They were covered with forests of oak and pine. A great river called the Klamath wound through the mountains and flowed into the ocean. Along this river were scattered the villages of the Yurok, the Karok, and the Hupa tribes. We will visit a Yurok home.

Little Yurok lived with his father and mother in a cellar house dug out of the earth. Over this dug-out room Yurok's father had built a roof of rude planks split from a fallen tree. He had split these planks with a wedge made of elk-horn. He drove the wedge with a pear-shaped stone maul. The roof was not flat. It had two ridges.

The cellar room was warm and comfortable in cold weather. To enter it the Indians crawled through a round hole in the lower end of an upright plank in the end of the house. The hole was only two feet wide. A short passage and a notched plank ladder led down into a square room five or six feet deep. There was a hole in the center of the floor for the fire. Above the fire one of the roof planks was propped up to let the smoke out. Of course it didn't all go out. Around the fire were stools for the family, and wooden pillows for their heads.

Here little Yurok's mother cooked the food, and here the family ate and worked. At night the mother and children slept here around the fire. The Yurok father slept in the "sweat house." This was another house which was a sort of smoking and sleeping club for the men of the village. It was called the "sweat house" because it could be made very warm so that the Indians would sweat freely. When they were wet with perspiration they would rush out and plunge into a stream. They thought this was a good way to cure illness and keep well.

Along the sides of the cellar room, on the ground level, was a shelf space. Here Yurok and his brothers and father kept their tools. Here Mother Yurok stored dried salmon and the big baskets of acorns from which acorn meal was made. Here, carefully folded, were the precious deerskins that Father Yurok wore in the ceremonial dances. These dances were held two or more times a year. They were religious dances—a kind of worship.

Ordinary deerskin clothing was there, too, ready for the family to put on when it was needed. In the warm days of summer, Yurok and his father and his small brothers and sisters wore no clothing. His mother wore only a little skirt of buckskin, fringed at the edge. In winter, when the weather was rainy and chill, they all wore deerskin capes. Each cape was made of two whole skins, with dangling legs. Mother Yurok wore lovely chains of shells. She had one chain of obsidian. The shiny pieces were cut so that they glittered in the firelight.

These Indians wore nothing on their feet. Yurok's father had moccasins, but he did not wear them about the village. When Yurok saw his mother getting out his father's moccasins he knew his father was going on a hunting trip. The moccasins had no thick soles such as our shoes have. Each moccasin was made of one piece of deerskin with a seam up the front and another up the heel.

6

When Yurok's father was going to hunt, Yurok's mother squatted on the ground and bound the moccasins on his father's feet with strong cords. She told Yurok to climb the ladder and reach down his father's quiver of arrows. The quiver was made of skin with the fur side turned in to protect the points of the arrows.

Of course Yurok's father took his bow, too. The bow was beautiful. It was made of yew, and was more than three feet long and about two inches wide. It was very thin, not more than half an inch thick. It was backed by deer sinews, painted with red and blue triangles. The cords also were of sinew. All the Yurok men made fine bows. They were proud of their careful work. Indians from other tribes came to buy Yurok bows. They brought things the Yuroks wanted to exchange for the bows—puma skins or the hard black obsidian from the mountains.

The arrows in the quiver were small and neat, with slender foreshafts of hard wood. They had tips of flint or obsidian. Yurok was learning to make such arrows. He was eager to be old enough to go hunting with his father.

Once his father had come back from the hunt with a white deer. What rejoicing there had been! A white deerskin was the most rare and valuable thing a Yurok Indian could possess. It took long strings of fine dentalium-shell money to buy one. Only the rich men and the big chiefs had them. The owners of white deerskins could take part in the White Deerskin Dances that were held in the fall and spring of the year. Yurok wondered if he would ever be lucky enough to kill a white deer.

When Yurok's father and the other men were away at the hunt, Yurok and his brothers fished in the river for salmon. They built a frame of poles which hung out over the river. Up in this frame they would sit for hours, watching the silvery fish go by beneath them. Down below in the water Yurok had spread his net. Through it ran a cord the end of which was fastened to a bone button in his hand. When a salmon swam into the net, jerk! Yurok drew the cord, and pulled up the net with the salmon in it. He struck the salmon

The Yuroks lived in plank houses

with a stout club. This killed it quickly. That night Yurok's mother would bake it in the fire for supper. When there was a big catch, the extra salmon were split and smoked or dried in the sun for winter food.

The Yurok people made heavy canoes by hollowing out fallen redwood tree trunks with fire. These dugouts were clumsy boats, but they served very well for crossing the rapid river. The Yuroks did not venture far out on the ocean, but they often paddled along the shore.

At the shore other kinds of food were to be found. There were mussels to be gathered and surf fish to be caught. Some-

They hollowed logs to make their boats

times a whale came near enough to be killed. Then the whole village took to their boats. They surrounded the strange sea beast, and hurled harpoons with loose bone barbs. When the whale was dead, it was dragged to shore and cut up. There were big slabs of meat for every family, some to eat at once and some to dry and put away for later use.

In the autumn Yurok and his brothers and sisters helped their mother gather acorns. Mother Yurok and the girls carried the acorns in deep cone-shaped baskets on their backs. The bands that held the baskets went around the girls' foreheads. They wore caps woven like baskets, to keep the cords from hurting their heads. They had to gather acorns enough to fill all their baskets over and over. A store of acorns for the whole year had to be put away.

After the acorns were gathered, they were spread out to dry in the sun and air. Then they were put into large storage baskets and placed on the shelf inside the house. When it was time to use them, the children helped their mother crack them. They helped to take out each round kernel with its sweetish-bitter taste.

Then came the grinding. Mother Yurok did this on a hard smooth slab of rock with a stone pestle about a foot long, shaped almost like a rolling pin. Around the acorn kernels on the rock she placed a hopper, or basket without a bottom. This kept the kernels together while she rolled and pounded them into meal. When the meal was fine enough, she brushed it from the rock into a basket. For brushing, she used a soaproot fiber brush. She sifted the meal through a basket woven for that purpose. She put the sifted meal into a hollow in the sand. After that she poured boiling water through the meal three or four times. This took out the bitter taste, and it was ready to cook.

For cooking, Mother Yurok used a special kind of basket, woven very smooth and tight, so that it would hold water. Into the water she put the meal, and dropped in hot stones from the fireplace. The stones were so hot they made the water boil and this cooked the mush. The meal with the stones in it had to be stirred all the time. Because of this stirring, the basket was not burned and the mush was cooked evenly. Mother Yurok stirred the mush with a paddle made of smooth red manzanita wood.

Sometimes the Indians ate the acorn mush while it was thin, like soup or porridge. Sometimes it was made quite thick. Then when it was cold it could be cut in pieces and wrapped up to take on a journey. It was very nourishing food.

In winter Mother Yurok had plenty to do making baskets. These were twined on hazel shoots. There were different shapes and sizes for different purposes. For some baskets she used split roots of pine, redwood, or spruce. These made coarse baskets for carrying heavy loads or storing foods. For others she used fine split roots of willow or grapevine, with woven-in patterns made of shiny bear grass or glossy, dark maiden-hair ferns. She made tight, smooth baskets for cooking and

11

for plates from which to eat, fine-stitched baskets for gather·
ing small seeds, beaters to knock the seeds into the baskets,
trays for sifting acorn meal, and fancy baskets for carrying at
the dances. She made a slipper-shaped basket to hold the baby.
When he sat in it his little feet hung out through two holes.

While Mother Yurok wove baskets, Yurok and his brothers
made fish nets. Their sisters drew long silky fibers from iris
leaves. The boys twisted these together two by two, and then
twined them into a two-ply cord. From this cord they knotted
their nets. Along one edge of the net, they fastened grooved
stones for weights. Each boy hoped to catch some big salmon
in his net.

Now let us leave the Yuroks and visit some Indians who
lived in the south.

Hundreds of miles away, on the coast and islands of southern
California, lived the Chumash Indians in their round houses.

The Chumash house was built of willow poles set in a large
circle. Their tops were fastened together in a small circle,
leaving a smoke hole in the center. Over the willow poles
were bound mats woven of tule reeds. The Chumash house
was very large and sheltered several families.

Little Chumash and his friends found tule reeds, for the
house mats, growing along the edges of streams, or in low
marshy places where the winter rains stood. They brought
them home by the armload every day, for each Chumash
mother found them very, very useful.

12

Mother Chumash made many things from these long pliable stems. From them she wove the mats that roofed their house and other mats to hang inside and divide it into rooms. She wove mats for bedding. These were spread on platform beds at night and rolled up out of the way in the daytime.

She used reeds also in making baskets. These baskets were coiled, not twined, like those of Mother Yurok. Mother Chumash used three reeds as a foundation. She coiled them around and around in a growing circle, sewing them, as she went, with fine threads of plant fiber. Never were baskets more carefully made than those of Mother Chumash. They were buff in color, with patterns of black outlined with yellow or white. She made many shapes of baskets, even one in the shape of a lovely graceful water bottle.

Mother Chumash cooked acorn meal in baskets, just as Mother Yurok did. But Mother Chumash had also fine cooking bowls of soapstone. There were large quarries of this soft smooth stone on the island we now call Catalina. The Indians who lived on the island carved this stone into bowls.

When a boatful of Indians from the island came paddling to the shore of the mainland the Chumash children came running and shouting. They wanted to see the things the island Indians brought to trade—stone bowls, brilliant shells, robes made of bright bird feathers.

The father of little Chumash had a fine boat, much like the boat of the island Indians. He had made it with the help of some of his friends. They felled a tree by building a fire at its

13

base. They split the trunk into rude planks by using wedges made of whale rib with blades of shell and wooden handles. They fitted the planks together into a flat-bottomed boat with high ends. They made holes in the planks and lashed them together with thongs of deer sinew. They filled the cracks and holes with a kind of oily pitch or asphalt, found in certain places in the ground or along the beach.

Such a boat as this would hold twelve people. Some of the men in the village had even larger boats. Little Chumash loved to go with the men when they went out on the ocean fishing. They caught fine large fish—yellow-tail and bonita.

The Chumash wove houses of reeds

Sometimes they let the little boy work one of the double-bladed paddles.

Chumash found plenty of interesting things to do. The beach was always strewn with curious shells. Many of them were the kind of clamshells that his people made into money. They broke the shells into pieces, and rubbed the pieces on stones until they were smoothed into disks or buttons. They made holes in them and strung them on cords. Chumash was making himself a fine string of money beads.

Sometimes he gathered pitch. He knew places where it seeped out of the hillside in a thick black trickle. He collected

They built strong boats of planks

15

it on flat stones or large shells and took it to his mother. She used it to stick her acorn hopper to the flat rock. When the rainy season was near she spread it over the mats of their roof to keep the house dry inside.

Sometimes in the late summer the Chumash men had a rabbit hunt. They chose a broad sloping meadow and set fire to the dry grass. The rabbits would leap out of the brush before the running flames. Many would be caught, and there was a great feast afterward. Chumash could remember once when the wind changed and blew the fire toward the village. Every house was burned to ashes. That was not so pleasant. But there was plenty of willow and tule. It did not take long to build more houses.

On the warm plains and inland valleys of southern California lived many tribes of Shoshone Indians. Their way of living was very much like that of the Chumash people, although each tribe had certain special customs of its own.

Now we will leave the Southern Indians and visit a Central tribe.

Between the mountain ranges of California was a broad and long valley. Through this valley, from the north and from the south ran two great rivers, which met and flowed into a great bay. This warm central valley was the home of many Indians—the Wintun, the Maidu, the Miwok, the Yokuts, and other tribes.

The Yokuts people, like the Chumash in the south, lived in

a house made of willow poles. But the Yokuts house was not round. It had straight sides and a peaked roof and was shaped something like a wedge. It might be a long house sheltering several families, each family with its own door and fire. Or it might be a separate house in a straight row of little houses. It was covered with tule mats, and had earth on top in winter to keep it warm. In summer it was hot in the great inland valley. So little Yokuts and his family moved into the open for the warm weather. They made a light shelter roof of branches. It was open at the sides and was held up at the corner by poles.

Mother Yokuts twined baskets like those of the Yuroks in the north, and she coiled baskets like those of the Chumash in the south. She used fibers of sedge roots, which were the color of earth. She made patterns with black fern root and crimson redbud bark. Fine designs ran in straight or broken bands around the baskets.

Her large carrying baskets were loosely woven and smeared with sticky stuff to keep them from leaking. She also made carrying nets, light and strong, with braided cords to bind them on her forehead. The string from which these nets were made was of shredded milkweed stems. Mother Yokuts rolled the fibers together on her thigh with her hand and then twisted them into a two-ply cord.

She stored the acorns for winter in a large container about three feet across. It looked like a big shaggy nest of brush and sticks twined together. It was fastened to upright poles, and hung a foot or two above the ground. Little Yokuts and

17

all his brothers and his sisters worked very hard to fill up the acorn nest.

In the cold nights of winter the Yokuts children slept under a warm blanket of rabbit skin. To make this blanket Mother Yokuts cut fresh rabbit skins into narrow strips. As they dried, these strips curled into ropes with the fur outside. The mother wove these furry ropes into a blanket that was thick and soft.

Mother Yokuts made a little pottery. But it was very crude. It was not decorated, and not even baked. She did not use it for cooking. She cooked in baskets or in pots of soapstone, carved out with sharp pieces of quartz.

The Yokuts boats were rafts made of tules tied together in

The Yokuts boats were tule rafts

tight bundles. These bundles were formed into flat boats, very long and a little higher at the ends. They were so light that they floated high on top of the water. These rafts would hold several people. They were moved with light wooden paddles. Little Yokuts liked to lie along the side of the boat and paddle with his hand. The Yokuts people used these boats to cross streams or to float out on the lakes or wide marshy rivers in search of fish or waterfowl.

There were many things in which all the California Indians —Northern, Southern, and Central—were alike. In winter they all wore the skins of deer or puma, the furs of seal or sea

Their reed houses were wedge-shaped

otter. They all paddled about on tule rafts, and wove rabbit-skin blankets. They all prepared acorn meal, for oak trees grew all over California. They all ate eagerly of fish, and of the meat of deer, rabbits, and wild fowl. In the forests and valleys of the north and central parts, food was more plentiful than on the warm dry plains of the south. The Indians in this southern part ate whatever small animals they could find, even snakes and grubs. They thought roasted grasshoppers very good food.

All the California Indians used many kinds of seeds as food. Through the lowland plains and the foothill meadows, when the grasses were yellow, the Indian mother would wander. Under one arm she carried her broad seed basket. With the other she swept the tops of the grasses with her woven seed beater. The small seeds showered into the basket. Hot stones, stirred in the cooking basket, toasted the seeds for eating. There was tender young clover to gather in the spring. There were wild berries in the summer and nuts in the fall.

All the California Indians made baskets—very good ones. The most unusual and brilliant baskets were made by the Pomo Indians, who lived not far from the coast north of the great bay. Their gift and dance baskets were decorated with black wavy quail plumes or scarlet woodpecker tufts, in gay patterns. Some had small beads woven in or fringes of shells

Through the greater part of California there was little or no pottery made before the coming of the white men. East of the mountains, however, in the great deserts reaching to the

20

Colorado River, lived the Mojave and the Yuma tribes. These Indians made excellent pottery, bowls of all sizes, and large ollas, or jars, to hold water. From here to the coast, on the southern edge of California, the Indians made pottery.

As in most Indian countries, the greater part of the work was done by the women. The men hunted. Because food was so plentiful, the California Indians did not need to be great hunters. They shot deer and elk and rabbits in the valleys. They snared wildfowl in the swamps and mountain lions in the canyons. But they were careful to let the great grizzly bears alone. They had plenty of time to rest and tell stories about the animals they hunted or the plants that gave them food.

The California Indians were a peace-loving people. Sometimes two villages quarreled over the right to fish in a certain stream, which they called a "salmon water." But they seldom had a battle. Quarrels were settled by a meeting of chiefs who talked the matter over. If there was fighting it was followed by a council meeting in which the dispute was settled. In some parts of the country money was paid, after a battle, for each person killed.

Often one village visited another to celebrate certain days or seasons. At these times there was not much feasting, but there was a great deal of dancing.

The California Indians did not roam about. Each group kept to itself, within well-marked boundaries. Trade was regularly carried on between Indians of different sections. Coast

Indians traded dried fish and shell money to forest Indians for acorns and animal skins.

Besides the dentalium-shell money of the far north, and the clamshell disks made all along the coast, there were other kinds of money. The Pomo Indians, who made the feathered baskets, made the most money. They took the hinges and curves of large clamshells and polished them into beautiful long pieces. They found in their country a kind of soft rock which we call "magnesite." They rubbed or ground this into cylinders from one to three inches long, pierced like beads. They baked these, and the heat turned them pink and red and brown. Handling made them glossy. These were worth more than shell money, as with us gold is worth more than silver.

As you can see, the California Indians were an easygoing, peaceful race. They had their own customs and laws, many of them very wise and sensible. They governed themselves quietly and traded with each other peacefully. There were times when a long drouth withered the growing things and caused the wild animals to die. Then the Indians suffered from hunger and sometimes from thirst. But for the most part their beautiful land gave them enough to eat and to wear without much work. They were a free and happy people.

Discoverers and Explorers

+‡+

Columbus and Cortes

FOUR OR five hundred years ago most of the white men in the world lived in the countries of Europe. The most thickly settled of these countries were along the shores of the Mediterranean Sea. One of these countries, as you know, was Spain.

One day there came to the court of Spain an Italian seaman called Christopher Columbus. Columbus had a wonderful plan. In old books he had read of men who thought that the earth was round. He believed this was true. He said that if it was true he could sail a ship straight west around the world.

Now most of the people of that time thought that the earth was flat. They said that if a ship sailed too far out on the ocean it would come to the edge and fall off. They were sure Columbus was talking nonsense! But Isabella, the Queen of Spain, was interested. She listened to all that Columbus said.

"This is an amazing thing," she said. "By sailing west could you reach India, which lies far to the east?"

"I am sure I could," replied Columbus. "Help me to make this voyage and I will find a way for ships to sail to the Indies."

Queen Isabella thought about this. Her eyes sparkled. From India and China and the islands of the East came rich silks, gold, jewels, and rare spices. They came by slow camel trains across Asia, and then by ship across the Mediterranean. They passed from one merchant to another. All this traveling took months, or years. It made things from the far East very costly. If Spanish ships could sail straight west to the countries of the East they could bring home large cargoes of rich things. It would mean great wealth for Spain.

"I will help you," said Queen Isabella to Columbus. "You shall have money to buy three ships and food for your sailors."

So Columbus set sail with his little fleet, steering straight west across the Atlantic Ocean. They sailed for weeks, seeing nothing but water. The sailors grew frightened. They thought they would never get back home.

"This man is crazy," they said to one another. "Let us throw him overboard and turn back to Spain."

But Columbus calmed their fears, and persuaded them to keep on. At last, more than two months from the time they started, they reached a little island. How good it was to be on dry land again! The weary captain and his sailors were grateful. They named the island San Salvador. This was in October, 1492.

Columbus believed he had landed on an island near the coast of India. He called the dark-skinned natives Indians. From this island he sailed to other and larger ones not far away. He noted that they were warm, pleasant lands much

26

like Spain. Then he sailed back home in triumph with his news.

The Spaniards were greatly interested in the discoveries of Columbus. The next year a number of people sailed back with him and settled on one of the new islands. They gave it the name of Española. It is now called Haiti. Columbus made several voyages. He drew charts of the islands, and he sailed along the mainland near them. He was looking for the cities of India and China which he felt sure were not far off. He found only wild country and dark-skinned savages. But when he died a few years later, he was still sure that he had found a new short way to India.

The rest of the world soon learned that Columbus was mistaken about this new land. Other ships sailed across the Atlantic—ships from Portugal, England, and France, as well as from Spain. The captains made maps of these strange shores and brought the maps back to Europe. They were very poor maps. The islands and continents shown on them were too large or too small, or they were in the wrong places. No two maps were alike. But they all showed one thing clearly. There was a new continent reaching from north to south across the ocean, blocking the way to India. This continent began to be called America. To reach the lands of the Far East the ships must find a way around or through America.

In this new game of exploration, Spain had the best of it. Spanish people settled on the islands of Española and Cuba, close to the new continent of America. Spanish ships started from these islands and followed the coasts of the mainland. Spanish explorers led their men through the forests of this mainland. They explored the part that we now call Central America. One explorer, named Balboa, climbed a mountain on the narrow isthmus of Panama and looked out on a great new ocean beyond America.

Then a sea captain named Magellan, in another Spanish ship, followed the coast of South America far down almost to its end. There he found a narrow stormy passage through which he sailed into the great new ocean. The passage through the strait was so stormy that the ocean seemed very peaceful. So Magellan called it the Pacific Ocean because *Pacific* means *peaceful*.

Across this great ocean he sailed for many days, until he came at last to the islands of the Far East. These were the islands for which Columbus had looked in vain. They really were near India and China.

Magellan lost his life in a battle with the natives of the islands. But his men sailed his ship on across the Indian Ocean and around Africa until they reached Europe again. They had sailed around the world. Now people knew surely that the earth was a globe. The new way to India had been found.

While Magellan's ship was crossing the Pacific, other Spanish explorers were searching the shores of America for rich lands and treasure. They found them in the country called Mexico. Here lived a race of Indians known as the Aztecs. They had palaces and temples built of stone and

28

carved cedar wood. They wore rich furs and beautiful cloaks woven of bright feathers. They had wide fields in which they planted corn and beans, pumpkins and bananas. They had shining chains and ornaments made of gold. The gold came from their own mines.

News of these things reached the islands of Española and

Cortes' March to Mexico

Cuba, and Spanish soldiers were sent in ships to conquer the Aztecs. Their leader was a brave young officer called Hernando Cortes. Cortes was bold and clever. He landed with his men and with sixteen horses in the harbor now called Vera Cruz. He sent the frightened natives with messages to Montezuma, emperor of the Aztecs.

Montezuma sent back gifts. But he warned the strangers not to come to Mexico. The way was long, he said, and beset with dangers.

29

When Cortes received the gifts and the message he laughed.

"This chief is afraid," he said. "Behold these gifts! His land is rich indeed. No dangerous road can keep me away."

Some of the men did not wish to march into a wild country full of savages. But Cortes was determined to go. At night he burned nine of his ships, leaving only one. In the morning he spoke to his men.

"All who are afraid," he said, "may take the last ship and sail back to Cuba. I shall go on to conquer Mexico. Those who dare may come with me to riches and glory."

"On to Mexico!" shouted the men.

The march began. The natives fled before them. They had never seen horses before, for there were no horses in America at that time. They thought the Spanish horsemen were strange monsters, part man and part animal. The guns terrified them. The white men, they said, were fighting with thunder and lightning!

Cortes conquered the Aztecs in a cruel war. He captured the beautiful city of Mexico. He took the lands and treasures of the Aztecs to enrich himself and his companions. He made himself the governor of the land and and changed its name from Mexico to New Spain.

But still Cortes was not satisfied. Surely there were richer lands beyond. He built ships on the western coast of New Spain and sent them out from the harbors of Tehuantepec and Acapulco. He wished to explore the western shores of this new continent of America.

So the ships of Cortes sailed along the coast of New Spain in the Pacific. There were islands not far away, some small ones and one very large one. Cortes learned that the Indians on this island dived for pearls. He believed that it must be a rich island.

A sailor named Ulloa was the captain of one of the ships of Cortes. Ulloa sailed up the stormy water between the mainland of New Spain and this large island. He found that it was not an island at all. Its coast drew close and joined the coast of the mainland. It was a long rocky peninsula, a part of the American continent. He took possession of it for Spain.

In this way what is now Lower California came to be claimed by Spain. Ulloa was killed before his ship returned to the harbor of Acapulco. Cortes went back to Spain, never to return.

CHAPTER III

✛✛✛

The Discovery of California

SPAIN WAS now indeed a rich and powerful nation. She had more ships sailing the sea than any other nation. These ships were called "galleons." They were large vessels for those times, with full square sails and with high ends having two or three decks.

The galleons sailed to the Spanish colonies in America bringing letters and supplies and more Spanish people to live in New Spain. They returned carrying gold from the mines of the New World. Other Spanish galleons made their way far to the south, sailed through the strait Magellan had found, and went on across the Pacific to the East Indies.

It was not easy to make a long sea voyage in those days. It was hard to be sure of having enough food. Often storms blew the ship from its course and the voyage took longer than the owners had expected. Then food gave out and everyone on board was in danger of starving. Sometimes the beans and biscuit and meat spoiled, or the sailors fell sick of scurvy from lack of fruit and vegetables. Often many died.

For these reasons the rulers of Spain were not satisfied.

They wished to find a shorter way for ships to sail to India. The Strait of Magellan was too far south. Surely there must be a passage through America farther north. They called this passage that they hoped to find the Strait of Anian. Every sea captain was told to look for such a strait.

New Spain was governed by a viceroy sent from Spain. The first viceroy of New Spain was called Mendoza. Like Cortes, Mendoza had heard of cities of gold and lands of treasure beyond New Spain. A book was published in Spain not long after the voyage of Columbus. In this book the author described a wonderful island called California, full of pearls and gold. Sailors had seen pearl divers in the islands west of New Spain, so they called these islands "the Californias." The largest one had turned out to be a peninsula and not an island at all. But still they called it California. And the stormy water which divided it from the mainland of New Spain they called the Gulf of California.

Mendoza had been told to search for the Strait of Anian. He wondered what lay north of the islands and the peninsula of California. He resolved to find out. A fleet of ships lay in the western harbor of Navidad. All he needed was a good captain to command them. He sent for Juan Rodriguez Cabrillo.

"They tell me you have sailed this Pacific Ocean," he said to Cabrillo. "And that you are a man of sense."

"I know this coast and these islands," replied the sturdy seaman. "And I can use my head."

"Can you obey orders?" asked Mendoza.

"I do my best, señor. Tell me what you wish me to do."

"I will give you two ships," said Mendoza. "Sail north along the coast of the Californias. Watch the shore line with care. See if the land is fertile. See if it is inhabited. Above all, see if there is a way to sail through it eastward to the Atlantic."

It was June of the year 1542 when Cabrillo started north with his two little ships. He had good sailors and plenty of food. He took with him as cabin boy a bright Indian lad from New Spain. From June until September he kept his ships headed north. It was very slow going against the hard north-

Cabrillo sent his cabin-boy to the Indians

west winds. He watched carefully but he saw nothing of a passage through the land. The sailors were very tired. Some of them were sick, because the food was spoiling.

One day Cabrillo saw an opening into the land. The two ships sailed through it, and dropped anchor in a protected bay. On the shore dark people were running about. Cabrillo's men launched the small boats. They could hardly wait to land. They all talked at once.

"Now for fresh water! We'll fill these empty casks."

"Food, too! There should be fruits at this season."

"Fresh roasted deer meat!"

He wished to make friends with them

"Or wild fowl! I can taste it now!"

When Cabrillo and his men landed on the shore, the Indians had vanished. They were hiding behind the bushes and in the hollows. Suddenly Cabrillo called his Indian cabin boy to him.

"Boy," he said, "go to those Indians. Perhaps you can speak their language. Tell them we will do them no harm. We come as friends."

The boy walked slowly toward the thicket, where dark forms could be seen. He held his hands out in front of him, palms up in friendship. Slowly and fearfully the Indians came out of hiding. They gathered around the lad and made signs to him. Presently they darted away. The boy came back to Cabrillo.

"They cannot understand me, señor," he said. "They speak an unknown tongue."

That night some of the sailors came back from the ships in a small boat to fish. A band of Indians shot at them with arrows. One of the sailors was wounded.

Cabrillo and his men stayed for six days in this bay. They gave the Indians beads and other small gifts, but they were still afraid of the white men. One day a severe storm came up. A gale blew from the southwest. But the two ships rode safely at anchor. Cabrillo wrote down in his record that this was a "safe and good harbor" for ships. This harbor is now called San Diego Bay.

It is interesting to know that white men discovered this

harbor in 1542, just fifty years after Columbus found the New World.

Then Cabrillo sailed north again and landed on the island we call Catalina. Here the Indians were friendly. They came out to the ships in their canoes. Leaving the island, Cabrillo and his men sailed across to the mainland. They saw the smoke of many Indian fires. Perhaps the Indians were having a rabbit hunt. They named the place the Bay of Smokes. This may have been San Pedro Bay.

The two ships followed the shore. They saw Indians fishing in their boats. They visited many villages of round houses, on the mainland and on the near-by islands which we now call the Santa Barbara Islands. They stayed for a week at anchor in a harbor of one little island, because it was too stormy to go on. This island is now called San Miguel. Here Captain Cabrillo fell and broke his arm. He had no thought of turning back, but started north again. Where was the Strait of Anian? There must be a large river which would carry them inland.

Now it was December. The weather grew worse. The winter winds blew hard and cold, and rains lashed the sea. Cabrillo found another bay that looked like a good harbor. It lay in the arm of a long point of land covered with rugged pine trees. But the sea was rough and the waves were high. The wind beat the ships about and they could not make a landing.

Cabrillo turned south and made his way down the coast to the little island harbor, for another rest. The hardships of the voyage and the lack of proper care for his broken arm were too much for the brave captain. He fell very ill. One day he called his pilot, Ferrelo, to his side.

"I shall not live to find the Strait," he said. "You must go on, Ferrelo. Chart the shores, search out the Strait, and take the word back to Mendoza."

The brave Cabrillo died. His men buried him there on the little island. But his grave has never been found.

Ferrelo sailed the two ships north through storms and against the wind for a long way. He went as far as the mouth of the Rogue River in what is now the state of Oregon. Then he was forced to turn back to New Spain. Of course he did not find the Strait of Anian, for there was no such strait.

But Cabrillo and Ferrelo had done much for Spain, and for the new land of California. They had sailed along eight hundred miles of coast. They had shown this to be the coast of a great mainland and not a group of islands, although there were small islands along its border. They had found no water-way through America for a long distance to the north. They brought news of one safe and good harbor for ships.

After Cabrillo's voyage the long peninsula near New Spain was called Lower California. The coast north of it was called Upper California.

✠✠

Ships on the Pacific

WHEN THE Spaniards under Cortes conquered Montezuma, they captured Mexico City and took possession of the country of the Aztecs. Then they set about making it a settled part of the Spanish king's domain.

After the soldiers who conquered, came the friars who taught. These friars set up missions, and made friends with the Indians. They gave them presents of food, cloth, and beads. They taught them the Christian religion. They persuaded many to live near the missions, to cultivate the fields, to learn trades, and to be good Spanish subjects.

In this way the Spanish rule spread in all directions. New Spain reached from the Atlantic to the Pacific. It spread farther and farther north toward the Rio Grande. Slowly it covered the country that we today call Mexico.

The Indians in the north were hard to subdue. This part of the country was rough and mountainous and far from Mexico City. Here were the rich gold mines. The Spanish were determined to hold this section. They made the natives work for them in the mines. The Indians hated this. Again and again they revolted, killing friars and soldiers alike. But farther south the Spanish rule was more successful, and the Indians were peaceful. New Spain became a valuable part of Spain's possessions. From her harbors on the Pacific, ships sailed to India and the rich Eastern lands.

While Mendoza was viceroy of New Spain he sent a fleet of ships across the Pacific Ocean to the East Indies. A group of islands was found and named the Philippine Islands after Prince Philip, the son of the King of Spain. Later, when this Philip became the king, he wanted to own the islands which had been named for him. He ordered that Spanish soldiers should go in ships and take them for Spain. This was done. The natives were conquered, and a Spanish colony was planted on the islands. This made it easier for the Spanish traders to get the things they wanted from India and China.

Each year a ship sailed from the port of Acapulco in New Spain across the Pacific to the Philippines. In this ship went merchants and traders to bring back silks and jewels, rugs and gold and spices. They could sell these things for high prices in Europe. The ship was called the Manila Galleon, because Manila was the capital city of the Philippines.

When the Manila ship returned to New Spain the fine things it carried were unloaded in the port of Acapulco. Long mule trains bore them across New Spain, winding through the mountain passes. In the harbor of Vera Cruz waited other Spanish ships to take them over the Atlantic Ocean to Spain.

Sometimes storms wrecked the Manila ship and its treasure

was lost. Sometimes pirates captured it and seized the gold and jewels. But every year without fail a galleon started from New Spain to make the voyage to the Philippines. And this Manila Galleon was one of the reasons for the settling of our California.

There was a strange thing about this voyage across the Pacific and back. The ships could not return by the way they had gone. A little south of New Spain the winds blew straight west across the Pacific. They filled the square sails of the Spanish galleons and carried them across the wide ocean in good time. But it was not so easy coming back. Then the winds were *against* them, and the galleons could not face such strong winds. They were blown back again and again.

The only possible way to return was to go north with the winds that blow along the islands of Japan. Farther north the winds did not blow steadily against them. So the captains could steer their ships east across the Pacific toward America. When they saw branches of trees floating in the sea they turned south. The branches meant that the California coast was not far way. The captains did not dare sail close to the coast. Storms might dash them against a rocky shore and wreck their vessels. In this part of the Pacific the winds blew hard from the north. These winds bore the ships quickly down the coast to New Spain.

Every year for two hundred and fifty years a Manila Galleon made its voyage to the East Indies, and came back in a half-circle to the north and down along the California coast.

41

Other ships, too, were sailing the Pacific Ocean. There were ships from England and from Portugal, Dutch ships, Russian ships, and ships that flew only the black flag of the pirate. Every sea captain had to look out carefully for the safety of his ship and its cargo. If the cargo was valuable, his ship was always in danger.

Spain was still the strongest nation on the sea. But England's power was growing fast. The two nations were bitter rivals. Each wished to rule the ocean, and their ships often met in battle on the high seas.

Sometimes an English gentleman of wealth bought a ship and set forth to look for riches and adventure in far countries. Such a captain was Francis Drake of England. He planned to defeat and plunder Spanish ships. Then he would be praised and would be rewarded by England's proud queen, Elizabeth.

Thus it happened that Drake came sailing up the coast of California in the year 1579, thirty-seven years after the voyage of Cabrillo. Drake's ship, the *Golden Hind,* was heavy with treasure. He had taken this treasure away from Spanish ships and colonies in the Pacific. Other Spanish ships waited to capture him when he returned south through the Strait of Magellan.

"We will sail north and find the Strait of Anian," he said to his men. "That will be a quick, safe way home to England."

Just as the rest had failed, so Drake failed to find such a strait. He looked for a place to land. His ship needed care.

His sailors needed fresh food and water. It would be a long voyage home around the world.

He found a bay where he could make a landing. Historians are not sure where he landed. It was far north of Cabrillo's island. It was probably at the place now called Drake's Bay. Here Drake and his companions built a rude shelter for themselves.

The Indians were friendly. They made the white men welcome and brought them herbs and feathered crowns. Drake

Drake's ship "The Golden Hind"

and his men made a journey over the hills. They found it "far different from the shore, a goodly country and fruitful soil, stored with many blessings fit for the use of man." They stayed more than a month on this shore.

Drake called the land New Albion. Albion was an old name for England. He set up a stout post with a brass plate on

43

it telling the date on which they came there. A sixpence bearing the head of Queen Elizabeth was fastened to the post. It
could be seen through a hole in the brass plate. Then they
boarded their ship and sailed away across the Pacific on their
homeward voyage.

Years passed by again, twenty-three years this time. Another
viceroy of New Spain, the Count of Monterey, received a
letter from the King of Spain. The letter said, "There must
be a port where my Manila galleons can stop for repairs on
the way home from the East Indies. The sailors need rest and
food and fresh water on so long a voyage. Send explorers at
once to find such a port in California."

The viceroy sent for Don Sebastián Vizcaíno, a daring and
skillful seaman who had sailed many times on the Manila
galleons. He made Vizcaíno commander of a fleet of three
ships, the *San Diego,* the *Santo Tomás,* and the *Tres Reyes.*
He sent him to California to find a port and to search again
for the Strait of Anian. Besides his sailors and soldiers
Vizcaíno took with him some friars of the Carmelite order,
and a good mapmaker.

He set out from Acapulco in May, 1602, and followed the
course Cabrillo had taken sixty years before. The record he
brought back was much plainer than Cabrillo's. We know
exactly where Vizcaíno went, because of his good maps of
the shore line. He set down names for all the bays, capes, and
islands. Today most of them are called by the names he gave
them.

44

Vizcaíno found and entered the "safe and good harbor" which had pleased Cabrillo. He named it San Diego for his ship. He was delighted with the port and the country around it.

The Indians were more friendly than Cabrillo had found them. The soldiers and friars gave them strings of beads and some biscuit and fish. Every day they came back for more presents. They tried to speak the Spanish words they heard the sailors use and they did it very well. They brought Vizcaíno and his men skins of wildcats and seals and small fishing nets of twisted fiber string.

After ten days, the ships left the harbor and sailed northwest against the wind. Father Ascension, one of the Carmelite friars, called this Northwest wind the "King and Master of this sea" because it gave them so much trouble. They entered and named San Pedro Bay, but they did not land there. They did land, however, on the island of Santa Catalina which they named.

The Indians there received them with joy and brought them fresh water from a distant spring in woven reed "barrels." The Spaniards set up their church tent and the friars said Mass. Throngs of Indians came to look and listen. They showed the white men their round houses, their boats, their harpoons, and their feathered robes.

Vizcaíno's fleet sailed along the channel between the islands and the mainland. Ever northward they went. A fog shut down and hid the shore for a time. When it lifted, high cliffs stood close to the sea. Beyond them a river flowed down from wooded hills. They named it the Carmel River in honor of the Carmelite friars.

Just beyond, reaching out into the sea, was the pine-clad point which Cabrillo had seen. Around on the north side of the point was a curved bay. The three ships dropped anchor. There was no storm now such as beat upon Cabrillo. Eagerly the tired voyagers left their ships.

Upon the shore stood a huge oak tree, stretching its giant branches to the very edge of the tide. Twenty paces away a ravine opened, and good springs of water bubbled out of the

Vizcaíno named the harbor Monterey

46

rock. Vizcaíno named the harbor Monterey, after the viceroy of New Spain. The whole party encamped on the shore.

Many of the sailors were sick with the scurvy. Sixteen had died and been buried at sea. Vizcaíno said that the *Santo Tomás* must go back to New Spain with the sick men. The other two ships would sail on to the north. He wrote letters to send to New Spain in the *Santo Tomás*.

He wrote in glowing words. The harbor was fine and easy to find. It had everything the Manila ships would need. "There are pine trees for yards and masts, very large live oaks and white oaks for building ships, and a plentiful supply of

The tired voyagers left their ships

sweet water," wrote Vizcaíno, "The port is well protected from all winds; the country is well settled with Indians and is very fertile. Climate and soil are like those of Spain, and whatever seed may be sown will produce a crop. There are great pastures and many kinds of animals and birds."

These were strong words of praise for the Bay of Monterey. It really was not "protected from all winds." But no doubt it seemed very comfortable to the weary seamen and friars.

The *Santo Tomás* sailed south with the sick men and the letters. The *San Diego* and the *Tres Reyes* sailed north. It was hard going against the wind. More of the sailors fell ill and died. The two ships became separated. At last, however, all three of the ships, with their maps and records, came once more to the harbor of Acapulco in New Spain.

There is one surprising thing about these voyages to California. Three great explorers had sailed along the coast, searching for a harbor and for a passage through America. Not one of the three, Cabrillo or Drake or Vizcaíno, had found the greatest harbor of all.

The Bay of San Francisco lay undisturbed behind the great rocky steeps of its narrow gateway. Perhaps fogs hid its entrance from the seamen as they sailed up the coast. Perhaps storms carried the ships out to sea just as they approached. Whatever the reason was, no one had found it.

The Missions

The Missions

CHAPTER V

One Hundred and Sixty Years

AFTER VIZCAÍNO'S voyage California was forgotten. There was war in Europe, and the King of Spain had his hands full. He changed his mind about wanting a port in Upper California. For more than one hundred and sixty years no ship landed on her shores.

On the eastern shore of America this was a busy time. Important things were happening. Ships came from England and from Holland. They brought people who wished to make homes for themselves in the New World. In the northern part farmers settled and cleared their acres. Little villages appeared and grew into towns and cities. In the south, cotton plantations spread over the countryside, and fields of corn and of sugar cane.

These colonies grew and spread farther inland. Steadily the white people pushed back the Indians and took more land. The eastern colonists were mostly English people, and the colonies belonged to England. They were ruled by governors sent from England.

North of these English colonies, in Canada, French people

settled. Hot disputes arose between England and France about their rights in the new continent. These disputes resulted in a war which lasted several years. When the war was over, France was defeated. All her possessions in America were surrendered to England. This was in 1763. England claimed all the eastern half of the continent of North America, extending to the Mississippi River.

The western half of the continent, beyond the Mississippi River, was a wilderness. Here herds of buffalo ranged, and Indians roamed through the forests. Vast plains, rugged mountains, trackless deserts stretched away to the Pacific. South of this western wilderness was the land of New Spain, ruled by viceroys sent from Spain. Spain's control covered Central America, and almost all of South America.

The viceroys of New Spain were making their land a settled and peaceful place. The friars worked patiently with the Indians. They followed the Rio Grande up into the wilderness beyond their country of New Spain. They planted missions among the peaceful pueblo Indians. They built churches and founded towns—Santa Fe and Albuquerque.

The most troubled spot of all New Spain was called Sonora It lay in the northwest corner toward the Colorado River. A famous Jesuit friar named Father Kino worked for years to start missions in this region. If this part of New Spain could be subdued, Upper California would be nearer. Over and over, a start was made. Then the fierce Apache or Comanche Indians would rise in warfare. The missions would be burned.

52

Friars would be murdered. It had all to be done over again.

Missions were started on the barren rocky peninsula of Lower California. They did not fare very well, because the land was so poor. Nothing would grow. But the Indians were peaceful there.

The beautiful coast of Upper California, *our* California, seemed to be entirely forgotten. But the maps and records of the explorers waited for the time when they would be needed. And sometimes in the schools and convents of old Spain the friars told again the stories they had heard or read of California and of the Indians who lived there.

✛✛✛

The Coming of the Friars

IN THE little town of Petra on the island of Majorca, close to old Spain, lived a boy by the name of José Serra. José's parents, Antonio and Margarita, were poor laboring people, but honest and respected. They often took the boy to church and to a convent in the village.

In this convent lived a group of friars of the Order of Saint Francis or San Francisco, as the Spanish called him. They wore robes of coarse grey cloth and went barefoot. They spent their lives studying religion, preaching and teaching, and helping the poor.

Antonio Serra was well liked by the good friars. When the small José came to the convent with his father, the friars made much of him. They taught him to read and write and to understand Latin, which was the language of the church services. He learned the chants, and often on feast days the convent Latin master took his pupils to sing with the choir.

José enjoyed these services and loved the friars. He wished very much to wear a grey robe and go about doing good as they did. But he was too young as yet. He was a quiet boy,

54

small for his age and not very strong. He loved to study. So his parents decided that he must have more education than the friars could give him. At the age of sixteen they sent him to Palma, the capital city of the district, where there was a large university.

Serra took up his studies eagerly and learned rapidly. He did not forget his desire to be a friar. At the convent he had heard of California far away across the sea. He wanted nothing so much as to go to the New World to teach the Indians of California. Before the year was over, he put on the grey robe of the Franciscan Friars and became a student member of the order.

José went on reading and studying. The books he liked best to read were those that told about the friars of earlier times. Some of these friars lived such good and noble lives that they came to be called "saints." José knew the stories of the saints by heart, and often told them to other boys who were studying at the convent. His favorite story was that of Brother Junípero, the friend of Saint Francis. Brother Junípero was a laughing, lovable soul. He was so eager to help the poor that he had to be watched or he would give everything in the pantry to those who came begging for food. One day he was caught stripping the beautiful lace from the altar "to sell for money to give to the poor."

When José's year of preparation was over and he became a regular member of the Order of Saint Francis, he changed his name from José to Junípero. He hoped to be as useful and good as the beloved Junípero whose story he knew so well.

Junípero Serra was such a good student that the friars put him in charge of classes of younger boys, and he taught for several years. Two of the boys he taught were Francisco Palou and Juan Crespí. A close friendship sprang up between the three, which lasted all their lives.

Years passed by. The three friends were busy preaching and teaching. Like the other friars, they were called "Father" by those with whom they worked. Father Junípero Serra was thirty-six years old when his chance came. A company of Franciscan friars were going to New Spain and a place was made for him. To his delight his dear friends, Father Francisco Palou and Father Juan Crespí, were allowed to go also.

Three months later they reached the harbor of Vera Cruz on the coast of New Spain. They were to go to the College of Friars in the city of Mexico, more than two hundred miles from the harbor. Serra wished to go on foot all the way. Palou went with him. The two made the long journey safely except for one thing. Father Serra's leg began to itch and burn. The trouble might have come from a mosquito bite. He scratched the leg in his sleep and made it very sore. This caused his foot to swell and give him a good deal of pain. It seemed a small thing at first, but it was never cured and troubled him all the rest of his life.

Serra and his friends were not yet to go to California. They were sent to work in the missions in the north of New Spain.

56

Twenty years passed. It was a long time, but Serra was not impatient. He was learning how to manage missions, and how to teach Indians. The time came when he was sent to the peninsula of Lower California. He was put in charge of all the old missions there. His heart was full of joy. He was closer than ever to the land of Upper California, of which he had dreamed so long.

About this time a man by the name of José de Gálvez came to New Spain. He was a powerful officer called a *visitador*. He had been sent by the King of Spain to help the viceroy, whose name was Croix. Gálvez and Croix talked over their problems.

"There are rumors on all sides," said Croix, "that the Russians are sending ships down the coast of California."

"I have heard this," said Gálvez. "They want furs. There are fur-bearing animals in California. It would not surprise me if the Russians plant a colony in California."

"We should build a fort at the harbor of Monterey," said Croix.

"We should have built one long ago," agreed Gálvez. "I have been thinking about the matter. I thought we could send a force to Upper California from Sonora. But I find it cannot be done. The distance is too great. There is a wilderness to cross, and the Apache Indians are fierce and not to be trusted."

"Have you any other plan?" asked the Viceroy.

"Yes, I have," replied Gálvez. "I am going to Lower Cali-

57

fornia. I will visit the missions there, and talk to Gaspar de Portolá who is governor of the province. He will know whether it is better to send soldiers and friars up the peninsula by land or to send them in ships. Perhaps we will do both."

Just at this time a letter came from the King of Spain. He, too, was thinking of Monterey and the Russians. "The ports of San Diego and Monterey must be occupied and fortified," said the letter. "We cannot have Russians or other foreign foes in our land of California."

Gálvez found Governor Portolá interested and ready to help. He promised soldiers and supplies, and he said that he himself would go with them to California.

But Gálvez knew that this was not enough. He must send men who would not get discouraged when hardship came. They must be men who would teach the Indians how to be good Spanish subjects. He sent for Junípero Serra.

Serra was fifty-six years old. He was a thin little man, and he did not look very strong. He was still lame in one leg. When he heard the plan for California he was so happy that he cried. The wish of his boyhood was coming true at last. He was going up into California to teach the Indians. His friend Crespí was going with him. His other friend, Palou, must stay and take care of the old missions in Lower California. But he would come later.

Everybody worked with a will getting ready. There were four parties of travelers, two going in ships, and two by land with cattle and horses and mules.

58

"You will start a mission in each of the ports, San Diego and Monterey," said Gálvez. "And a third in between, on that pleasant shore near the islands. It shall be the mission of San Buenaventura."

Serra went from mission to mission on the peninsula collecting whatever each could spare for the new missions. He needed vestments and linens and candles for the church services, pictures and crosses and candlesticks and church bells, and gifts for the Indians.

Governor Portolá gathered together the animals. Gálvez ordered the supplies—dried meat, flour, wheat, raisins, figs, sugar, lard, pack saddles, implements, and seeds.

Then came the packing. The *San Carlos* lay ready in the harbor. What a bustle there was! Gálvez worked as hard as anyone. He carried things on board the ship with his own hands. Serra checked off the list of things for the Mission San Carlos of Monterey. Gálvez gathered those which were meant for the Mission San Buenaventura.

"I'll get my things packed first, Father," he said with a laugh. And when he did he was delighted.

In January, 1769, the *San Carlos* set sail in charge of Captain Vila. With him went Captain Fages, with soldiers from Spain. In February sailed the *San Antonio,* commanded by Captain Pérez. He was a brave, hearty old seaman who had once been captain of a Manila Galleon. Gálvez promised to send a third ship, the *San José,* as soon as possible, with more food and supplies.

In March Captain Rivera started up the peninsula by land, with twenty-five soldiers. These were stout men used to the frontier life of New Spain. They were often called "leather-jackets" because they wore short coats made of tough hides. Besides the soldiers there were more than forty Christian Indians from the old missions of Lower California, and Serra's good friend, Father Crespí. They drove with them a great herd of animals—two hundred cattle, one hundred and forty horses, forty-six mules—with heavy packs of wheat and corn, dried meat and fruits, and other food.

Last of all went Governor Portolá with Father Serra, more native Indians, and some soldiers led by Sergeant Ortega. All these men starting by land or sea had a part to play in the story of California. We shall hear of them again and again.

Before Father Serra started north he visited Palou.

"I leave these missions in your care, dear friend," he said. "How I wish you were coming with us to Upper California! You will come someday."

"I hope so," said Palou with tears in his eyes. "This thing I will do. From now on I will keep a record of all that goes on in the missions of Upper California. Send me letters telling all that happens where you are. Our friend Father Juan Crespí will keep a diary and send it to me. It is important that we have these records. The day will come when men will wish to know about all these things, just as they occurred."

It was a long hard journey by land from Lower California to Upper California. The peninsula up which they traveled was a desert country, with few growing things and very little water. It was rocky and steep in places. Father Serra went on foot like the others, although his lame leg was painful. One day the pain was so great that he could neither stand nor sit.

The mule driver treated Father Serra's lameness

The governor had the Indians make a litter and carry him. It grieved Serra to give trouble to others. That afternoon he called to him one of the mule drivers.

"My son," he said, "you know how to take care of your animals if they are hurt. Don't you know how to cure my leg?"

"I know nothing about medicine," answered the poor man. "I am only a mule driver, Father. I can cure the sores on the backs of the pack animals, but that is all I can do."

"Very well, then, my son," said Serra. "Pretend that I am

one of your beasts of burden. Make a remedy and apply it just as you would to an animal."

The mule driver laughed and the rest joined in. "I will do it to please you, Father," he said.

He crushed a little tallow, and mixed it with some herbs which he had found growing in the fields. This he heated and put on the swollen leg and foot. That night Serra slept well, and the next day his leg was better and he could walk.

In July, 1769, all four parties met at last on the shore of San Diego Bay. The *San Carlos,* which had sailed first, had been blown from her course. She reached the bay long after the *San Antonio* had arrived. All her sailors were sick, and many died after reaching land. The *San José* had not arrived.

Captain Portolá knew that he must march on to Monterey and start to build the fort there, as he had been told. He wished to send one of the ships to Monterey with food and tools. But one ship must go back to San Blas, the harbor of New Spain, for more supplies.

"The *San Carlos* cannot sail without sailors," said Portolá. "She must stay here in port. Captain Pérez, you must take the *San Antonio* back to New Spain for food and more men. We must go on. Perhaps the *San José,* the third ship, will meet us at Monterey. We must take the chance that it will."

Father Serra stayed at San Diego to care for the sick and make friends with the Indians. Governor Portolá marched away to the north to find the harbor of Monterey.

✠✠

The Lost Port of Monterey

GOVERNOR PORTOLÁ took with him on his march to the north the men who were strong and well. Captain Rivera, Sergeant Ortega, and Lieutenant Fages had thirty-four soldiers in all. Father Crespí and another friar had two servants. There were fifteen Christian Indians from Lower California and seven mule drivers to care for the pack animals. Sixty-four persons started out that sunny mid-July morning to go to the port of Monterey.

They wound along the broad valleys. To their left sparkled the sea, to the right rose the hills. They camped each night beside a spring or small stream. Father Crespí wrote in his diary all that took place each day. They did not travel fast. On some days they covered only four or five miles, on other days ten or twelve. Often they rested for a day while a few rode ahead to find the best way to go.

The Indians were friendly. They came in large numbers from their villages of reed huts. They brought food to the white strangers, and Governor Portolá gave them strings of beads.

The first two weeks the party traveled about one hundred miles. "Now we are coming into the country where the rivers begin," wrote Crespí in his diary.

At the end of July they camped beside the river that is now called the San Gabriel. On the second of August they came to another river which they named the Porciúncula. It is now called the Los Angeles River. Here they pitched their camp in a pleasant valley in a grove of cottonwoods and sycamores.

Crespí noted the rich land for planting grain and seeds. It was the best place for a mission that he had seen. Indians from a near-by village brought them reed baskets full of roasted seeds and chains of shell beads. This was the village of Yang-Na. It was here that the city of Los Angeles would be founded twelve years later.

The following day the march was to the west over a wide plain. Camp was pitched in a grove of alders near a large spring. Crespí called the place the "Spring of the Alders of San Estevan." There were marshes near by, of a substance like pitch, boiling and bubbling in the water. These oily marshes are called today La Brea Pits. They are near Wilshire Boulevard in Los Angeles. From these famous asphalt beds, scientists have taken the skeletons of thousands of animals of ancient times which had drowned there.

On went the governor and his company, day after day. They crossed the hills to the north and the wide valley beyond. They followed the Santa Clara River to the ocean. On the

64

shore and on the islands not far away, they found many Indian towns. The Indians gave them fresh fish, caught from their rough boats.

They kept along the seacoast to the northwest until they came to the high white cliffs of the Santa Lucía Mountains. They turned inland around this rough region and came back to the coast down another river valley. This, they thought, must be Vizcaíno's Carmel River, and Monterey must be close by! But when they reached the shore they were confused and disappointed. There was a point of land covered with pine trees, to be sure. But it was *south* of the river! These pine trees were not tall and straight and suited for masts! Surely that little stream below the point could not be the Carmel! This could not be the famous bay! This shore was uneven with sand dunes! The governor called a council. The friars and officers gathered about him.

"What shall we do?" asked Portolá. "It is now October. We are all weary. Many are sick. Our toilsome journey seems in vain. Let each speak his mind."

One by one they spoke.

"Surely it must be farther on."

"We cannot give up now."

"How can we turn back and confess that we have failed?"

"Thank you for your courage and loyalty," said Portolá. "We will go on. We will yet find the port."

For three weeks more they pushed their way up the coast. Looking ahead, they could see the bay where Drake had landed and the great rocks called the Farallones. Then they knew they had passed the harbor of Monterey.

Wearily they made camp. Portolá and Rivera were both ill, and many of the others also. Young Ortega was sent with a few soldiers to explore the country.

"If you catch sight of the *San José* with its cargo of food," said Portolá, "it will mean that our lives are saved."

When Ortega came back a few days later he had a strange thing to tell. They had found a great arm of the sea stretching into the land for miles. They had started to march around it, and had discovered that it was too large. It was San Francisco Bay, the great harbor which all the explorers had missed.

When Portolá's men reached the coast

Portolá was bitterly disappointed. He was not interested in a great inland sea. His soldiers were sick and starving. He wanted only to find the port of Monterey and the supply ship which he hoped would be waiting there.

The next day they broke camp and turned south, coming back to the Point of Pines that they had passed. Again they explored on all sides. Again they decided this could not be the famous port. On the south side of the Point they set up a large wooden cross. On it they wrote, "Dig at the foot and you will find a letter." Buried in a bottle was a letter telling of their search and their return to San Diego. A second cross was set up on the north side near the bay.

they did not recognize Monterey Bay

Wearily over the hills and valleys southward they trudged. They were hungry. Their food was nearly gone. The Indians had little to offer them, as the fishing season was over. On the twenty-fourth of January they reached the Bay of San Diego. They had been gone more than six months.

Father Serra was sad. "I am sure you found Monterey," he said. "That must have been the place. Perhaps the Carmel River dries up to a small stream during the summer. Perhaps the port is not so good as we have thought all during these years."

Father Serra was discouraged too. He had built a hut for a church. He had hung up the bells brought from New Spain, and had rung them. He had held a church service and founded the Mission of San Diego.

All this he had done. But he could not make the Indians understand about the Christian religion. They took the presents of beads and cloth the white men offered. But they were still afraid. They kept out of sight, coming back only to steal what they could. They had attacked the little camp one day and wounded one of the friars in the hand with an arrow. They showed no desire to live at the mission or to become Christians.

Portolá found that the supply of food was nearly gone. The *San Antonio* had not returned from New Spain. Nothing had been seen of the promised *San José*. Then Portolá sent Captain Rivera back by the land route to Lower California for more food.

68

"We will stay just as long as we dare," he said. "The *San Antonio* may return any day with food for us. Surely the *San José* must be lost at sea."

The *San José* really was lost at sea. No one ever heard of it again. The weeks went by and no ship came. Portolá looked grave. He began to pack. He did not wish to go back to New Spain without finishing his task, but it seemed that he must.

Serra and Crespí talked sadly together. Would all their plans and hopes end in nothing? Day after day they prayed for the coming of the ship. The time was set for departure. On the very last afternoon, when hope was nearly gone— Look! was that a sail far out on the ocean?

Eyes were strained toward the horizon. Hope sprang up in anxious hearts. The hope turned to joy. It *was* a ship! The *San Antonio* came sailing into the bay. How excited everyone was! Good Captain Pérez had brought plenty of food, more men, letters from the King and from Gálvez—letters of cheer and praise.

Portolá made ready to start again for Monterey. This time they were determined to succeed. The *San Antonio* sailed north with supplies. Father Serra was on board. By land marched Portolá with Crespí and the soldiers and Indians. It did not seem far this time, because they knew the way. When they reached the Point of Pines they found the cross they had left covered with feathers and arrows and shells. These were gifts from the Indians to the God of the white men.

A few days later the *San Antonio* anchored in the bay. From the sea there could be no mistake. The bay looked just as Vizcaíno had said. They wondered why they had ever been in doubt.

Crespí had his own idea. "Our Father, Saint Francis," he said, "kept the port of Monterey hidden from us, so that we would go on north and discover his own harbor, San Francisco Bay. We will have a mission there some day."

Everyone fell busily to work building huts of branches. Father Serra hung his bells on the bough of a tree. One June day they rang the bells, fired their guns, and held a church service. This was the way the second mission was founded, the Mission of San Carlos of Monterey.

Portolá's work was done. He had started settlements at the two California harbors, a fort and a mission at each. He prepared to sail back to New Spain with Captain Pérez in the *San Antonio*. He put Lieutenant Fages in charge of all the soldiers. This really made Fages the governor of Upper California. Father Serra was the head of the two missions.

"But two missions are not enough in this great land," said Serra. "There must be many others, with a good road leading from one to the other. All the Indians must hear of the true God and of Jesus and His cross. They must learn to till the fields and raise food, to make clothes and build better houses. They must become a Spanish people."

Serra sent letters to Gálvez by Captain Pérez. He asked that more friars be sent to California, more soldiers, more

70

food and tools. "Send bells also," wrote Serra. "Bells must ring at each of my missions to call the people to prayer."

Back and forth went the good ship *San Antonio* on its long journey with faithful Captain Pérez. It brought soldiers for the forts and grey-robed friars for the mission work. It brought wheat and corn for bread, and seeds of many kinds for the mission fields and gardens.

Three new missions were started. Southeast of Monterey, on the eastern slopes of the Santa Lucía Mountains the Mission San Antonio was founded. Farther south, where Portolá had turned inland from the coast, Mission San Luis Obispo was placed. In the warm southern plain, "in the country where the rivers begin," was started the Mission San Gabriel.

This was done in the first three years after the Spanish had come to San Diego. Then word came that Gálvez had gone back to Spain. There was another viceroy in New Spain. A second piece of news meant a great deal to Father Serra. The old missions in Lower California would no longer be in the care of the Franciscan friars. So his dear friend, Palou, would soon be on his way to Monterey.

California's Chain of Missions

The Spanish Settlements

CHAPTER VIII

✠✠

Through the Wilderness with Anza

THE NAME of the next viceroy of New Spain was Antonio Bucareli. Bucareli was exactly the right man to carry on the work Gálvez had started. He was much interested in the California missions, and he understood the danger that threatened them.

It was hard to raise food in California. Seed had to be taken there from New Spain. There were not many people to work in fields and gardens. There was little rain, so seed had to be planted near streams. Sometimes it was planted too near and the stream overflowed and washed away the crop. Sometimes it was too far from the water, and it dried up. Food for the soldiers and the missions had to be sent from New Spain.

It took the supply ships months to go from the harbor of San Blas to San Diego and Monterey. Sometimes they were wrecked or driven out of their course. At such times the people in California nearly starved. True, there was a land trail up the peninsula of Lower California. But there was little food in Lower California to send. Supplies had to be sent there by ship across the Gulf of California. Crossing the narrow

75

gulf was dangerous. Many a ship was battered to pieces there by wind and waves.

It was plain to Bucareli that a new way to California must be found. Gálvez had thought of going to California from Sonora, the troubled northwest corner of New Spain. But this meant crossing a wilderness, with the threat of savage Indian tribes.

Rumor came again that the Russians were planning to come to California. More soldiers were needed to defend the country from foreign ships. People felt that there should certainly be a fort on the Bay of San Francisco.

"We cannot make a Spanish land without Spanish people," said Bucareli. "There must be other Spanish in California beside soldiers and friars. There must be families—fathers and mothers, and children who will grow up and have families of their own. These settlers could plant fields and gardens and raise food."

Bucareli appointed Captain Rivera, the man who had led the first land party to San Diego, to be the next governor of Upper California. He told him to gather more leatherjackets in the peninsula, and to take their families to California with them. He allowed Rivera to take other families, also—all who were willing to make the journey to the new country. Bucareli gave him careful directions about what to do as governor.

"Let no ships of other nations land in our California ports," he wrote to Rivera. "Take great care in choosing the place for each new mission. Some day these missions may become great cities. Explore the Bay of San Francisco at once. Find a place for a fort and a mission there."

One day about this time Bucareli received a message from a man named Anza. Anza lived in Sonora. He had traveled north from Sonora all over the country we now call Arizona. He knew it very well. He had been a great Indian fighter.

"We can travel from Sonora to California by land," said Anza. "I can find a way for many people to go, with horses and cattle."

This pleased Bucareli very much. "That is an excellent idea," he told Anza. "Go and map out this new way."

Captain Anza took twenty soldiers and two brave friars and rode away from Sonora into the northwest. They started with a herd of sixty cattle. They passed through the country of the fierce Yuma Indians. Anza made a friend of one of their chiefs. This Indian, who was called Palma, showed them great kindness.

In the desert wastes beyond the Colorado River, Anza and his party suffered from thirst, and their cattle began to die. They were forced to return to the land of Palma. Here they left part of the cattle and made a fresh start.

This time they were more successful. They marched around the great desert sand dunes. They passed through the mountains and reached the green slopes of California. At the mission of San Gabriel the friars received them with rejoicing.

Anza and his men went on to Monterey, but they did not stay there long. Gathering new supplies for the homeward

Wise and courageous was Captain Anza

journey, they turned back across the wilderness to New Spain. But they left behind them in California new hope and happiness. Anza had found a way from Sonora to the sea. People in California felt closer to New Spain than ever before.

Meanwhile Bucareli was doing something else for California. He sent four ships to take supplies to the missions and forts and to explore the northern coast. One of these ships was the *San Carlos,* which had carried the first friars and soldiers to San Diego. It was in command of young Lieutenant Ayala.

One August day in 1775 this ship sailed into the Bay of San

78

Safely he led his colony to California

Francisco, which was to be one of the great harbors of the world. Ayala explored the bay for more than a month. Then he sailed back to report to Bucareli that it was "not one port but many ports with a single entrance."

Bucareli was pleased with the news about the bay. He was even more delighted with Captain Anza's report. Now he could send settlers from Sonora to California, to build a fort and town on the shores of San Francisco Bay. He could send animals, too, which was very important. Herds of cattle, increasing in California, would save the country. He ordered colonists to get ready—all who wished to go. The very next

79

year Anza gathered his party and prepared to start again for California. With him went Lieutenant Moraga and Father Pedro Font. Father Font kept a diary of the journey.

There were two hundred and forty of the new colonists, men and women and children. Bucareli gave Anza money to buy everything they would need. Anza had money not only for food and clothing, but even enough to buy hats for the little boys and hair ribbons for the little girls.

Everybody rode horseback. Two or three children rode on one horse, or perhaps a child rode with his mother or father. Clothing and supplies were packed on the backs of mules. There was a long line of mules with drivers to guide and tend them.

The party took many things that were needed in California. They drove with them a large herd of cattle. Some say that on the back of one of the mules was a sack containing four cats for the mission fathers. The good fathers had complained that they had trouble with rats.

It was a long hard journey for so many people. The traveling was rough. The dust rose in choking clouds from beneath the feet of the horses. The first serious problem, however, faced them on the bank of the Colorado River. It was running higher and deeper than when Anza had crossed it before. It was too deep to be forded. After a search Anza found a place where the river divided and spread out into three shallower streams. These they crossed without difficulty.

Beyond lay the shifting, sandy desert. Across it howled the

bleak winds of winter. The mountains around the horizon were covered with snow. The people in Anza's party had come from a warmer climate. They suffered from the cold and from lack of water. Some of the mothers had wee babies to carry in their arms. But through rains and storms they crossed the mountain passes safely. So wise was Captain Anza, so careful in his planning, so thoughtful of the needs of everyone, that every person got safely through to California. Indeed, the party was larger when it reached California than when it started, for several babies were born on the way.

When they arrived at San Gabriel, Governor Rivera was busy with other matters. There had been an attack on the San Diego Mission. Indians had burned the mission building and killed the good friar in charge.

Captain Anza did what he could to help, but he could not delay his own work. He led his people to Monterey. Then he took Lieutenant Moraga, Father Font, and a dozen men north with him to explore the shores of San Francisco Bay.

They camped on the high slopes of the San Francisco peninsula, much pleased with what they found. Anza chose the table-land above the great gate of the bay for the location of a fort. He saw oak trees near by for timber with which to build it. Several miles southeast, near a spring and a little river, was a place well fitted for a mission. They called the little river Dolores. When these matters were settled, Anza departed for New Spain.

Lieutenant Moraga had been left in charge of the colonists

from Sonora. It was he who led them north in June to found the fort and mission of San Francisco. And who should go with the party but our old friend Father Palou! He had been in Upper California three years. He had made a trip to the bay region with Captain Rivera to plan for a mission there. Now he was eager to get things started.

On the high land near the entrance to the bay the fort was laid out. The *San Carlos* had brought the supplies for the new

Dolores Mission of San Francisco

settlement, and the sailors helped with the building. Walls were constructed of stout oak logs set upright. There was a storehouse, a chapel, a dwelling for the commandant. There were houses for soldiers, their families and the other settlers.

Beside Dolores River was built the mission church and a dwelling for the friars. Below stretched the waters of the great south arm of the bay. Here some day ships from all the

82

world would find harbor. Thus, in September of 1776, was founded San Francisco.

Here in Dolores Mission, Palou took up his work. Letters passed between him and his beloved friend, Serra. Sometimes the Father President of the California missions came to visit his old pupil and talk over mission affairs. Faithfully Palou kept his records. He collected the diaries of Crespí and other friars. He kept letters and accounts. He made notes of what happened in the missions and of ships that came to the ports.

The year 1775 was an important one on both sides of the American continent. In California, Lieutenant Ayala in the *San Carlos* was exploring the Bay of San Francisco. In Sonora, Captain Anza was gathering together his company of colonists and starting across the desert to California.

Meanwhile, on the eastern side of America the English colonies had decided not to be ruled by England any longer. They felt that many of the English laws were unjust to them. The governors sent from England were often harsh and unfair. The colonists wished to make their own laws and choose their own leaders. The year 1775 saw the beginning of the Revolutionary War. In this war the United States of America won freedom from England and became a separate nation.

We have not space in this book to tell the story of that great war. But it is interesting to see on one side of the continent the growth of California as a Spanish mission land, and on the other side the birth of the nation which would one day claim California as one of her states.

+++

Fort, Town, and Mission

THE SPANISH had a threefold plan for settling their new lands. They built forts, missions, and towns. The forts, or *presidios,* protected the land from foreign foes. The missions taught the natives the Spanish religion and the Spanish way of life. The towns, or *pueblos,* provided a place for settlers to live and cultivate the land.

The friars at each mission were expected to teach the Indians until they understood how to take care of themselves. Then the Indian village at the mission would become a pueblo like the others, with a church and a town hall. The friars would leave and go elsewhere to start new missions.

Bucareli was not satisfied with the way this plan was being carried out in California. The missions were not growing as he felt they should. Many of the Indians took no interest in them. So Bucareli appointed a new governor who he felt would take hold vigorously and get results more quickly. This new governor was Felipe de Neve. He is sometimes called the greatest governor California ever had.

84

When Neve reached California two more missions had been founded. One was San Juan Capistrano. It was located on the coast not far north of San Diego. The other, Santa Clara, was south of San Francisco near the lower arm of the bay.

Neve traveled through the whole of California, visiting each presidio and mission and taking note of what he saw. There were three presidios now, San Diego, Monterey, and San Francisco. There were eight missions, San Diego and San Juan Capistrano on the south coast; San Gabriel in the warm southern plain beside its river; San Carlos on the Carmel River near the Point of Pines; San Antonio and San Luis Obispo on the eastern slopes of the Santa Lucía Mountains; and Santa Clara and San Francisco on the great bay in the north.

Neve had in mind the need for raising more grain. As he journeyed the length of the land, he found two regions which would be excellent for this purpose.

One of these was the fertile valley at the southern end of San Francisco Bay near the new mission of Santa Clara. The other was not far from San Gabriel Mission on the rich southern plain through which flowed the River Porciúncula. This was the place Father Crespí had praised in his diary, where the Indians of Yang-Na lived among the trees, the roses, and the wild grapevines.

These two spots would be fine places to start pueblos. Here settlers could build homes and plant gardens and fields.

Neve lost no time in starting the first of these pueblos. From the presidios of Monterey and San Francisco he took nine soldiers who knew something about farming. He also took five families of colonists who had come with Anza. He chose a place near a river a little distance from the mission of Santa Clara.

A tract of farm land and a lot for a house was marked off for each citizen of the new pueblo. He was given a yoke of oxen, two horses, two cows, two sheep, two goats and a mule, together with seeds and farm tools. He was given a supply of food and ten dollars a month. These things he would repay with grain from his harvest. Houses were constructed, and a dam was built across the river with a ditch to irrigate the lands.

Thus in 1777 was founded the pueblo of San José. It was the first town in California that did not begin as a fort or a mission.

Not long after this, Bucareli died. In him California lost a great and wise friend. The work of caring for the California missions was carried on by General Croix, who was head of the northern provinces of New Spain. General Croix was a nephew of the Viceroy Croix who had worked with Gálvez for California.

General Croix wrote to Governor Neve that the Santa Barbara Channel had been too long neglected. It must have a presidio and several missions. A new pueblo on the Porciúncula River must be founded as soon as possible. He summoned

Captain Rivera to Sonora to collect soldiers for the new missions and presidio, and settlers for the new pueblo.

Captain Rivera set about doing this. He sent the settlers across to Lower California by ship. From there they went north to Upper California by the old land trail and reached San Gabriel Mission.

Captain Rivera himself started from Sonora by the Anza trail with a large company of soldiers with their families. When they reached the region of the Colorado River, where Anza had visited Palma, a terrible thing happened. Trouble had been brewing among the Yuma Indians for a long time. They were no longer friendly to the Spanish. Now the storm broke. The Indians fell upon two missions there. They burned the buildings and killed the friars. They killed many of the settlers and all the soldiers who were in camp there. Captain Rivera perished with the rest.

When the sad news reached California there was grief in the hearts of the friars. They were sad to hear of the death of those other friars. They were sad also because no longer was it safe for Spanish settlers or soldiers to come to California from Sonora. Once more the fierce and warlike Yuma Indians blocked the way.

But the other settlers were waiting at San Gabriel, and Governor Neve set the fourth of September, 1781, to found the second pueblo in California. On the appointed morning the twelve settlers and their families left the mission and marched nine miles across the sunny plain to the chosen place.

Father Serra's dream had come true

The lots were marked out around a plaza, or open square. There was a place for each home; and there were places for a guardhouse, for a storehouse for grain, and for a town hall. The settlers began at once to build the little mud-roofed houses and to dig ditches to carry water to the fields.

The little pueblo was given a very long name, *El Pueblo de Nuestra Señora la Reina de los Angeles de Porciúncula,* the Town of Our Lady the Queen of the Angels of the Porciúncula, shortened to Los Angeles, which means "the Angels."

No one at that time dreamed that this tiny settlement would one day be the fifth largest city in the United States. There was

88

The missions were busy, thriving places

no reason why anyone should. The United States itself could hardly be said to exist as a nation. The Revolutionary War was not yet quite over. Cornwallis surrendered at Yorktown six weeks after the first settlers began work at Los Angeles.

That winter, on the first day of the new year, Father Juan Crespí died. He had traveled the length of California exploring and writing in his famous diaries. Now he was laid to rest in the Mission of San Carlos—the mission where he had worked with his beloved Serra.

In the early spring Father Serra and Governor Neve founded the presidio of Santa Barbara. They founded also

89

the first mission on the Santa Barbara Channel, the Mission San Buenaventura. This was the mission that had been planned so long before when Gálvez and Junípero Serra packed the supplies for California in the *San Carlos*. It was the ninth and last mission to be founded under the care of Father Serra.

Missions now stretched in a chain down the land of California, as Serra had planned. The Indians had forgotten their fear of the friars. They had come to build their villages near the missions in great numbers.

Over the hills and through the valleys from mission to mission went a road. It was called *El Camino Real,* the King's Highway. It was not really a highway, only a well-worn dusty trail, beaten by the feet of men and horses. Along the King's Highway the grey-robed friars trudged on their mission errands, and soldiers rode swiftly with letters. Father Serra himself limped over it visiting the missions he loved.

For fifteen years Father Serra had watched his work growing greater and more beautiful. But Father Serra was growing old. In 1784 he went for the last time from San Diego to Monterey, pausing at each mission to bless his brother friars and the Indians he called his children. He was so weary and ill that he scarcely expected to reach San Carlos Mission. But he grew better, and was able to visit his friend Palou at San Francisco, and to stop at Santa Clara on his way home. In August Father Palou was called in haste to the Mission San Carlos by the Carmel River, to be with his friend and teacher in his last hours. Father Serra died on August the twenty-

90

eighth. He was buried near his friend Crespí as he had wished to be.

With Crespí and Serra both gone, Palou was lonely indeed. He longed to go back to New Spain. He laid aside the book he was writing about the missions, and wrote instead the *Life of Junípero Serra*. When he sailed for New Spain the next year he took with him both books. They are Father Palou's

San Fernando Mission

gift to us today, the true story of the beginnings of California and of the founder of her missions.

After this Father Lasuén became the head of the California missions. Father Lasuén did not have the fire and energy of Junípero Serra. But he was a wise man with a kind and generous heart. Not so much is known of him as of Serra. He had no lifelong friend to write down his life story. But he ruled the California missions long and well.

91

Besides caring for the nine already started, Father Lasuén founded nine more. Santa Barbara was beside the Santa Barbara Presidio, and La Purísima Concepción was out on the point not far away. Santa Cruz was north of Monterey across the bay; Soledad and San Juan Bautista were east of Monterey, and San Miguel south of San Antonio. San José was north of Santa Clara, on the east shore of San Francisco Bay. San Fernando was in the broad sunny valley north of Los Angeles. San Luis Rey was in the far south near San Diego.

Each of these eighteen missions had two friars to guide and teach the Indians and a guard of soldiers for protection. All were well started by the year 1800. This was only thirty years after Portolá and his band traveled from San Diego to San Francisco Bay searching for the port of Monterey.

A few years later the Mission of Santa Inés was founded, between the Santa Barbara and Purísima missions. A long time afterward two more missions were established north of San Francisco Bay, the missions of San Rafael and San Francisco Solano. They brought the number to twenty-one. The last two were not so large or so important as the others. They were founded too late to take a real part in the mission life of California.

✠✠✠

The Golden Years

THE YEARS just before and after 1800 are often called the Golden Years of California. This is because they were such happy peaceful years. The people of California did not know what was going on in the rest of the world. They had no newspapers. They received almost no letters or visitors from outside their own land.

California was a little world by itself. Only once in a long while did a ship drop anchor in the port of Monterey. The overland way from Sonora was not often used, because of the warlike Yuma Indians. The supply ships from New Spain were the only link with that country. They did not come oftener than once a year.

Life was carefree and gay. There was plenty of food. Each family had its own vegetable garden, its orchards of fruits. The mission fields of wheat and corn spread over the valleys. There were thousands of cattle on the hills.

At first there had been trouble with the Indians. Hostile tribes attacked the missions at night. They set fire to the thatched roofs. They shot arrows at the friars and at the Christian Indians. Sometimes they stole mission cattle or horses.

But as time went on there was less and less trouble. Thousands of Indians lived in peace and quiet at the missions. They grew used to the new way of life. They had to work hard, but they were fed and clothed. They learned to love the friars.

The missions were busy, thriving places, each like a little city. A mission was usually laid out in a large square or oblong, with the church at one corner. At first the buildings were constructed of wooden planks, with a fence of palisades, or stakes, surrounding the square. Gradually these flimsy wooden buildings were replaced by structures of adobe. Adobe was a kind of stiff clay. Large bricks, usually square, were made from it. These bricks were not baked in ovens, but were dried in the hot summer sun till they were hard enough to use.

The new churches were often built of stone, with beautiful arches where hung the mission bells. The roofs were of red tiles, bright in the sunlight. All these buildings were constructed by the Indians. The friars made the plans and directed the work. They remembered the churches and dwellings of Spain, with their simple beautiful lines. Most of the mission churches were amazingly beautiful for a land so far from the centers of civilization.

The mission inclosure was surrounded on the inside by a solid row of small rooms. These were the dwelling rooms of the friars and the workshops of the mission Indians. The Indians were taught various trades. They became skillful carpenters, brickmasons, blacksmiths. They learned to make

94

soap. They cut and sewed leather into shoes and saddles. Some of the leather articles they made were very beautiful. They pressed grapes from the mission vineyards into wine. They learned to play the violin, the guitar, and the flute, and to sing the chants of the church services. They herded the cattle and horses of the mission and worked in the fields and gardens.

Outside the mission inclosure was the Indian village, called the *ranchería*. Each Indian family had its own hut of willow boughs and tule mats. When the girls became young women they stayed at the mission, sleeping in a large room together at night.

The food for all the Indians was supplied by the mission. It was simple but wholesome. Their morning meal consisted of *atole,* a thick gruel of ground corn. Sometimes the corn was roasted before grinding, and a little *panocha,* or brown sugar, was added. Then it was called *pinole.* When cattle became plentiful some were killed each week, and the meat was divided among the Indians. This meat was roasted in pieces before an open fire, or made into a stew with beans, corn, peppers, or pumpkin. At certain seasons the Indians were allowed to go to the hills and gather the seeds, nuts, and wild fruits that they loved.

The friars rejoiced most of all that the Indians had become Christians. Always the church and its services were an important part of mission life. The sweet-toned bells rang for the worship of God every morning and evening. The Indians still sometimes held their native dances. But these were no

Sometimes a foreign ship dropped anchor

longer held as religious exercises. So the friars did not object.

The mission friars did not own the broad grain fields, the herds of cattle and horses. If you had asked them, they would have told you that all these things belonged to the Indians. They would have said that they had come only to teach the Indians how to use and take care of such things, and how to live like Spanish subjects. When the Indians were able to care for themselves the friars would give them the lands and cattle, some for each one, and the missions would become regular towns.

But the friars did not teach the Indians to take care of themselves and their property. They taught them to speak

96

The visitors were grandly entertained

Spanish and to work with skill at many things. But they thought the Indians were too much like children to manage their own affairs. Year after year they kept on caring for them as if they were children. They gave them food and clothing, planned their work, punished them when they did not obey, and rewarded them when they were good.

The friars felt that the time might come when some viceroy of New Spain would command them to give up the missions. They hoped it would not come soon, or perhaps that it would not come at all. They did not know what would become of the Indians if that time came.

Towns grew up around the presidios, at San Diego, Santa

97

Barbara, Monterey, and San Francisco. The town of Monterey was especially gay and lively. Here the governor lived and many soldiers had homes for themselves and their families.

Once in a long while an English or a French ship sailed into the curved bay. Then there was a grand ball for the visitors. The Spanish girls and women put on their finest dresses, full ruffled skirts, rich embroidered shawls, handsome jeweled combs, and lovely lace veils called *mantillas,* which they wore over their hair. The foreigners were entertained in grand style.

Besides those who lived in the pueblos or in the presidio towns, there grew up another class of people in California. They were the families of retired army officers. These officers were often well-educated Spanish gentlemen. When they retired, they were given grants of land by the king or the governor. They bought cattle from the mission herds. The land grants were called *ranchos;* the owners were called *rancheros.* The ranchos were usually very large. A Spanish ranchero could gallop on his horse for many miles and still be on his own land.

The herds increased until thousands of cattle grazed on the hills of the ranchos. These cattle were valued for their hides and tallow. The hide was the whole skin of the animal, stretched to dry, and then sold to be made into leather. The tallow was the fat. It was melted and poured into bags made of smaller skins. This also was sold. Spanish ships took the

98

hides and tallow when they brought supplies to California.

The King of Spain gave orders that the Californians must not trade with ships from other countries. But the Spanish ships did not come often. Later on, English and American ships sometimes landed at Monterey or at one of the other ports. They brought things the Californians wanted—silk and lace, tea and coffee, tools and dishes. The friars and rancheros secretly traded their hides and tallow for these things. Often they could get them in no other way.

The Spanish rancheros had large families. Many brothers and sisters and cousins sometimes lived in one large ranch house. These houses, like the missions, were built of adobe bricks, and the walls were very thick. The thick walls kept the house warm in winter and cool in summer. The rooms of the ranch house were often built around an open square. In the square was a garden or open court called a *patio,* with a fountain in the center, and covered porches around the sides.

The children of the *ranchos* did not go to school, for there were no schools. As time went on, many of the *rancheros* and their wives could not read or write. They were little concerned with books or study. They left these things to the friars. It was all playtime for them. The climate was so mild that they spent most of their days out of doors. The girls were taught embroidery and sewing and how to manage a house. The boys followed their fathers in raising horses and cattle.

Everybody rode horseback. There were thousands of horses. Little children learned to ride as soon as they could walk. The men were wonderful riders, and their horses were full of spirit and fire.

Most of the ranch work was done by Indians. The mission fathers sent the young Indian girls to live at the ranchos. The Spanish women could teach them, better than the friars could, how to do housework. The Indian men helped the rancheros with the cattle and horses. They were called *vaqueros*.

The ranchos were separated by boundary marks, not by fences. So the cattle from several ranchos would often graze together. Each ranchero had a brand, or mark, on his cattle to show which ones were his.

The most exciting event was the rodeo

The most exciting events of the whole year were the *rodeos,* or roundups. These were held twice a year, in the spring and in the fall. At this time all the cattle from neighboring ranches were driven together to be separated and counted. The calves were roped and each was marked with its owner's brand. This was done with a piece of iron bent into the shape of the brand and heated in a fire.

It was a lively time. The girls and women gathered to watch. The men rode through the crowding cattle on their spirited horses. What a noise there was! The cattle bellowed! The vaqueros shouted! The sun blazed down on the rising dust

The men were mounted on spirited horses

clouds. When the hot work was over, it was time for the feast. This was spread in the patio of the ranch house. Music, dancing, and laughter continued far into the night.

The Spanish young people loved to dance. They had scores of graceful and interesting dances. They celebrated everything with a party which they called a *fiesta*. They played games showing the skill with which they could ride. They sang gay songs, sometimes making up new verses. And always they danced—alone, in couples, or in groups.

The *ranchos* covered so many acres that the homes of the owners were far apart. They were as far apart as if the owners had lived in different towns. There might be a distance of thirty or forty miles between two *ranchos*. When people went to see their friends or relatives they stayed several days. Often whole families went visiting, to attend a wedding or celebrate a special feast day.

Any traveler going through the country was warmly received. At mission or ranch house the door was open to him. Food and a place to sleep were ready for him. No one thought of asking him for pay. Instead of that, money was placed in the guestroom. He might take what he needed. A horse was his for the asking. The whole countryside was a friendly place.

But there came a time when this peace and happiness was disturbed. In order to understand the reason for this we must go back to New Spain. Here the people had grown tired of the rule of the Spanish kings and of the nobles sent to govern them. They felt as the American colonies had felt under England's rule. They were not fairly treated and the Spanish kings demanded too much tax money from them.

Spanish colonies in South America were fighting for their freedom from Spain. New Spain joined in the revolt. The people chose leaders and clamored to change the laws and the government. They called their country by the old name of Mexico instead of calling it New Spain.

This dispute between Spain and Mexico turned rapidly into war. Because of the war, California was forgotten. The supply ships no longer came to Monterey. There was no money to pay the soldiers at the presidios. There were no new uniforms. Fortunately, the missions raised plenty of food. The friars sent supplies to the presidios, and allowed them to borrow what they needed. Nobody starved. But the gay, careless happiness was dimmed. There were complaints, arguments, worries, bitterness.

The people of California were too far away to get news quickly or correctly. They did not understand about the war. They expected the King of Spain to put down the revolt, and bring order to New Spain once more. Instead of that the King was defeated. Mexico became a free and separate nation.

The government of Mexico sent a ship to California to carry the news. It was announced that California belonged to Mexico and not to Spain. The Californians were surprised and not entirely pleased. But Spain, after all, was far away across the world. They could hope for no help from that quarter. It made little difference in California what flag flew over the port. The officials, therefore, promised to be loyal to Mexico.

The mission friars were the most disturbed by the change of governments. Many of them refused to take the oath of loyalty to Mexico. They thought that Spain would surely rise in her strength and take back her New World colony! If she did not, what would become of the missions, now grown so great and rich? The friars did not like the new rules laid down for them by Mexico. Some of them left California.

Things did not go smoothly in Mexico. The leaders began to quarrel among themselves. They paid no attention to the needs of California. The soldiers at the presidios were not paid. Governors came to Monterey who were not wise or good. The Californians disliked them. One was so bad they put him on a ship and packed him off to Mexico again.

They tried electing their own governor, but they could not agree. Part of the time there were two governors, one in the north and one in the south. There were outbreaks and plots. It was a restless time.

To make matters worse, the Mexican government sent orders for the friars to give up the missions. The missions had been in charge of the friars for fifty years. That was far too long, the government officials said. The missions must become pueblos and the friars must leave. This was called "secularization."

It was a bad state of affairs, the thing the friars had always dreaded. Governor Figueroa, one of the few good governors sent from Mexico, saw how impossible it was to secularize the missions. Not only would the Indians suffer, but also the soldiers at the presidios. All their food came from the missions.

Figueroa tried to arrange things so that the change would come slowly. But governors before him, and greedy officials had carried things too far. A man called an "administrator" was sent to each mission to close it and distribute the land. Some of these men enriched themselves and their friends with land and cattle.

It had always been understood that when a mission was closed, its property was to be divided among the Indians of that mission. In many cases this was not done, or was not fairly done.

The Indians were bewildered. Some grieved to have the friars leave. Others were glad to be free to go where they pleased. They made no plans. For the most part, they did not farm the land or care for the cattle. What they had was quickly lost or stolen. A few had married into Spanish families. A few others held together in small groups and made a new life, partly Indian and partly Spanish. But most of them gradually disappeared. Thousands fell sick and died. Others wandered away to their old wild life. But they were no longer fit for that, and they, too, died. All that the missions had done for them seemed to have been done in vain.

The breaking up of the missions took place—for the most part—between the years 1830 and 1840. That is, it happened during the time when Andrew Jackson and Martin Van Buren were presidents of the United States.

Some of the mission buildings were sold. Some were deserted and left to crumble slowly into ruins. Mission life in California was ended. The Golden Years were over.

Changing Times

CHAPTER XI

+++

Ships in California Ports

IN THE early days of the missions, Russians had founded a settlement in Alaska. Alaska was on the west coast of North America far north of California. The Russians had come to Alaska to hunt for animals with beautiful furs. These furs were very valuable.

Later on, during the Golden Years of California, a Russian ship sailed down the coast to San Francisco to buy food for the Alaskan settlers. The captain of the ship was pleased with the country. He took back a fine report. Other Russian ships came a few years later to plant a settlement there.

North of San Francisco Bay, on a high bluff near a river, the Russians built a fort called Fort Ross. It had strong walls and some good cannon. The river was called the Russian River. The Russians hunted fur-bearing animals in the surrounding country. They also hunted sea otters for their furs. There were many sea otters off the coast and in the Bay of San Francisco.

The Russians put up some good farm buildings and two or three mills. They made tools and other articles from iron,

109

wood, or leather. The Californians needed these things. They traded hides and tallow for them, and sometimes fruit and grain.

Meanwhile, on the eastern side of America, the new nation called the United States of America was growing rapidly. After the United States had won freedom from England she

Fort Ross

began to build up a trade of her own. She had to send out ships to bring the things she needed from other countries.

Nowhere could be found more shrewd and able seamen than the Yankee captains from the New England states. They sailed their ships far down around South America and into the Pacific Ocean. It was no longer necessary to go through the stormy Strait of Magellan. The Yankee captains had learned to go farther south, around the end of the continent. The farthest point was Cape Horn. Terrific gales blew in from the

110

Pacific around the cape. But it was safer for the ships to be out in the open sea than amid the winding rocky shores of the strait.

Around the Horn and across the Pacific went the New England trading ships. In the ports of China they bought tea and silk and spices. They discovered that the Chinese wanted furs. Their houses had no fires in winter and they needed furs to keep themselves warm. The wealthy Chinese would pay high prices for good furs.

When the American sea captains anchored in California, they found it an excellent place to get furs. While Spain controlled California, they had to keep out of the way of the Spanish officers, for these officers had orders not to allow any foreign vessels to trade in the California ports. But the American captains often succeeded in dodging the officials. They offered tempting sums of money to the Californians for furs.

In California they could buy furs of many kinds—rabbit, beaver, muskrat, fox, sea lion, and seal. Finer than any of these was the fur of the sea otter. The otters with the most beautiful skins were those caught in San Francisco Bay and around the islands of the Santa Barbara Channel.

Captain William Shaler in his ship the *Lelia Byrd* came into San Diego harbor early in 1803. After Captain Shaler and some of his men had been on shore, the commandant of the port came on board and told him that the Spanish laws forbade him to trade in the harbor. Captain Shaler and his partner, Richard Cleveland, talked it over.

111

"See here, Shaler," said Cleveland, "I've located a bunch of otter skins. The men who own them will sell them to us. We'll have to be careful. We can send a couple of boats ashore tonight after dark."

When night had fallen, the two boats put off across the waters of the bay. After some time one boat came slipping back to the vessel. Ropes were lowered. Low voices were heard.

"Did you bring the furs?"

"All safe. Pull up."

"Where's the other boat?"

"We don't know. Not so lucky. We heard a hail and a shot."

When dawn crept over the hills, Captain Shaler turned his glass on the shore. There was his other boat. There were his three men, bound and guarded. The captain took four men, each with a brace of pistols, and made a landing. He demanded the release of the captives. The guards let them go. The captain dipped the guns of the guards in water. Then he hurried his men into their boat and back to the ship.

But how was the *Lelia Byrd* to get out of the harbor without being sent to the bottom by the guns of the presidio? "There are eight brass nine-pounders, all in fair shape, at the presidio," said Captain Shaler. "I examined them myself. What's more, they have plenty of ammunition."

"Nothing to do but run for it," said Cleveland. "Look! Those guards have given the alarm. People are gathering!"

All sail was set, the anchor raised, the *Lelia Byrd* moved toward the entrance of the bay. Her three little guns and her

112

fifteen men faced the fort. Shots whistled through the air. One tore some of her rigging. One made a hole in her side, which was quickly stuffed up. Then the ship's guns opened fire. The first broadside sent the crowd of onlookers scampering. The second seemed to awe the fort into silence. Not another shot was fired. The *Lelia Byrd* took to safety.

This was not at all usual. Most often, Captain Shaler and the other traders of the sea found it very easy to get all the furs they wished. They slipped into the little coves along the shore of California. They bought furs from friars or soldiers or private citizens. They traded for them shoes, crockery, cotton cloth from New England, and shawls, spices, and gay handkerchiefs from the Orient.

Two years after the San Diego adventure, the *Lelia Byrd* was again on the California coast. She had been to China, and she was leaking badly. Captain Shaler anchored in the sheltered little harbor of Catalina Island and careened her. Her timbers were almost eaten through. It took more than a month to put her into shape. Shaler and Cleveland and the crew had plenty of time to enjoy the climate of the island. They made friends with the Indians, who seemed to like the Yankee sailors.

"It's a shame," said Captain Shaler to Richard Cleveland, "the way Spain handles a country like this. The idea of making it a crime to trade with other countries! Why, trade is the very thing California needs! If the United States owned this country, she would make it one of the finest on the globe. A

113

brisk trade and plenty of industrious settlers—think what they could do for a land with a splendid climate and with rich plains where anything will grow!"

"And what's more," continued the shrewd Captain, "it would be an easy job to take California. Spain has made it easy. She's opened up the country, planted it with grain, stocked it with cattle, and tamed the Indians. Easy for any nation to land and take possession!"

"What of the forts?" asked someone.

"The forts!" laughed the captain. "There isn't a fort on this coast that could hold out an hour against the guns of any fair ship-o'-the-line. Their guns are puny and their guards are few. What's more, the folks on those ranchos would be glad to get under the flag of a country that would make them rich. I'm going to write an account of California that will open some eyes back in Washington to what's out here."

Other Americans came to California. The sea otters were killed in such numbers that they disappeared entirely from the ocean near the coast of California. But something else brought ships to these waters. Whaling vessels began to come to hunt for the whales spouting not a great way from the shore.

These whaling vessels, too, were from New England. They were small ships. It took them a long time to make the voyage. They had to sail around Cape Horn, then north to the place where whales were found, and after that back to New England again. They needed a place to land where they could repair

114

their hulls and replace broken masts. The sailors needed fresh food and a chance to rest on land. Whaling boats began to enter California ports, seeking these things.

The captains of these whalers brought with them from the States the things that Californians wanted. They exchanged tools and dishes and other manufactured goods for fresh beef and green vegetables and fruit. They made little journeys into the country near the ports. Then they sailed back to the United States with stories to tell of the beautiful land of California where living was easy and comfortable.

Like the seals and sea otters, the whales were gradually killed or driven away from the California coast. But by that time the American sea captains had found out that California was a fine place to buy hides. The New England shoe factories needed hides for shoe leather. There were thousands of cattle on the great California ranchos.

After Mexico separated from Spain, California no longer belonged to that country. There was no law in force against trading with any ship that came. A good business sprang up. Ships from the United States dropped anchor often at Monterey, at San Pedro, at Santa Barbara and San Diego. The Californians called them the Boston Ships, because many of them came from the busy harbor of Boston.

Over the sunny plains down to the shore rumbled and squeaked heavy two-wheeled carts called *carretas*. Indians walked beside them, guiding the slow ox teams. Hundreds of hides from mission or rancho were piled up on the beach.

Great, stiff dry things they were, each one the skin of a whole animal, folded once in the middle.

Out in the harbor lay the ship, swinging at anchor. She could not come in close, for there were no docks. Back and forth from ship to shore plied the small boats manned by sailors. They carried the hides on their heads from the shore to the small boats. Then they rowed out to the ship with them. In the small boats, boxes came to shore full of things from New England—things greatly needed in California.

The *rancheros* and friars came to the shore on horseback. From the boxes they chose the things they wanted to change for hides. The sailors called the hides "California bank notes."

Boston ships entered California ports

SHIPS IN CALIFORNIA PORTS

If the landing place was good and the sea was calm, the sailors would row their Spanish customers out to the ship. In the ship's hold was a room fitted up like a store. It was a busy little store, and a gay one, when California came on board to buy from Boston.

Back sailed the ships around the Horn and north to the ports of the United States. The sailors were full of stories of California with its sunny days, its cattle and fields and vineyards. The people of the United States listened to these stories. What a good place to live that must be! But the sea voyage was long and dangerous. How fine it would be if there were a way to go to California by land!

Down to the shore rumbled carretas of hides

✚✚✚

The Coming of the Covered Wagons

ONE DAY a man came to see the Governor of California at Monterey. He said his name was John A. Sutter. He was a Swiss who had traveled widely. He had come to the United States to live when he was thirty years of age. Sutter had been a soldier. He wanted some land, so that he could start a colony and build a fort on the Sacramento River. With the fort, he said, he would help defend the land against the wild Indians in that part of the country.

"That is a good idea," said Alvarado, the governor. "We need a fort on the Sacramento River. But I am not allowed to give lands to anyone who is not a Mexican citizen."

"That's all right," replied Sutter. "I will gladly become a Mexican citizen."

Governor Alvarado sent for the citizenship papers at once. Just as soon as it could be arranged, John Sutter was given his land beside the river. It was a great stretch of country about eighty-five miles long. There was room for vast fields, great herds of cattle, homes for many people.

118

THE COMING OF THE COVERED WAGONS

About this time the Russians were ready to give up their fort on the Russian River and leave the country. The seals and sea otters and most of the fur-bearing animals that had lived on land were gone. Sutter offered to buy the Russians' cannons, their boat, and their other possessions. They were much pleased and sold him everything, even though he had no money at the time. He promised to pay them when he could.

Then Sutter built a strong fort on his Sacramento River land. He fixed up the old Russian cannons to guard it. He trained Indians for soldiers and for workers in his fields. He soon had many farm buildings. He also had a mill and a landing place on the river for boats.

On the other side of America, pioneers from the United States were pushing farther and farther west. They brought their families in covered wagons. They built new homes and turned forests into fields. Their farms and villages reached to the Mississippi River.

Long before this, England and France had fought for control of America. When that war was over, France gave up all right to the country east of the Mississippi. The unexplored wilderness west of this river was claimed by Spain.

But France wished to have a place in the new continent. French settlers had come to live at the mouth of the Mississippi River. This region was called Louisiana. In the year 1800, Spain—by a special arrangement—gave to France a very large tract of land in America. It reached from Louisiana up the Mississippi and Missouri River valleys.

This troubled President Jefferson. He was afraid the French might decide not to let American ships go down the Mississippi and out through the port at the river's mouth. He sent James Monroe to France to try to buy this land. The plan was successful. The great stretch of country was bought from France, in 1803, for $15,000,000. This was called the Louisiana Purchase. It included most of the region between the Mississippi River and the Rocky Mountains.

President Jefferson at once sent explorers to find out what this great new country was like. He wished to know if it were possible to get through it all the way to the Pacific Ocean. The explorers were led by two fearless young men named Meriwether Lewis and William Clark.

Following the rivers as closely as possible, they made the long difficult journey. From the head waters of the Missouri they crossed the Great Divide to the upper Columbia River. This they followed to the Pacific. The journey led them next through Oregon, the country bordering the Pacific Ocean north of California.

Before Lewis and Clark reached home again, more than two years had passed. They had a wonderful story to tell of their explorations. Books have been written about their adventures on the long journey. But we cannot give them much space in this story, for they did not enter California.

The success of Lewis and Clark encouraged other men to venture into the forests and plains of the West. These men were brave, hardy fellows who loved an out-of-door life. They came on foot or on horseback. Usually they were in search of beavers and other fur-bearing animals.

Some of these hunters were just as interested in exploring new lands and finding new trails as they were in trapping beavers. They did not mind steep mountains or burning deserts or narrow escapes from Indians if they succeeded in finding new country—country where no other white men had traveled.

One such explorer was a young trapper named Jedediah Smith. He is sometimes called the Pathfinder of the Sierras. With a party of men he explored much of the country west of the Rocky Mountains. In the summer of 1826 they made their way across the desolate wastes of Utah and Nevada. They were almost starving by the time they had left the desert behind. Crossing through a pass in the mountains they found themselves in California. Soon they arrived at the Mission San Gabriel.

The lean, hungry backwoodsmen, weary from the long trail, were amazed and delighted, when they saw the rich fields of the mission. The rolling hills had been watered by the first rains of autumn. Sleek herds of cattle grazed on the young green grass. It was a beautiful and cheering picture.

Father Sanchez, later President of the Missions, lived at San Gabriel. He was a fat, jolly, friendly soul, generous and hospitable. He welcomed the strange foreigners with their coonskin caps and deerskin jackets. He gave them cloth to make new shirts. He spread before them a feast such as they had dreamed of on their long nights of hunger. There were fat

121

roasted fowls and fish, potatoes, beans, and green peas, with red apples and purple grapes, and some wine from the mission press.

Jedediah Smith was told that he must go to San Diego to see Governor Echeandia, in order to get permission to travel through California. While he was gone on this errand his men waited for him at the mission. One of the men, Harrison Rogers, kept a journal. In it he wrote a record of the things that to him seemed strange and interesting.

Rogers enjoyed the music of the Indian band—two violins, a bass viol, a trumpet, and a triangle. He visited the mission soap factory, and saw four huge brick cisterns, with a kettle set in the bottom of each, holding two hundred and fifty gallons of soap. More than sixty Indian women were spinning yarn and others were weaving. At the mission he met a man from Boston by the name of Joseph Chapman. Chapman had built a mill for the Mission of San Gabriel. He had married a Spanish girl and built a home in the pueblo of Los Angeles. He told Rogers about a pitch mine that yielded forty barrels of pitch a day.

Some of Smith's men grew restless at the mission. They quarreled among themselves. They were not accustomed to an easy life. Probably they were glad when Jedediah Smith returned from San Diego.

He had fresh horses and was ready for a new start. The governor had told him to leave California. Smith was eager to explore this very pleasant land; so he chose the longest way

122

out. He decided to go north through the valley and then cross the high mountains to the east.

He led his men northward through the valley of the San Joaquin River. The snow was too deep in the mountains for them to get through. Smith left his party behind in camp and set out with two companions. They succeeded in getting through the snowy mountain passes and across the desert to Salt Lake. Here Smith gathered a new party of men and retraced his way to California and north to the camp he had left.

The combined party started north toward Oregon. Up the valley of the Sacramento River and over the mountains to the coast they went. They lost some of their horses in crossing swift rivers. They trapped fur-bearing animals in the valleys and took the furs with them. At the northern border of California the party was set upon by savage Indians. Almost all were killed, among them young Harrison Rogers. Only Smith and two others escaped and made their way home by the Oregon route. Jedediah Smith was the first American to travel the length of California from San Diego to the northern border.

Smith and Rogers were followed by others. The western country was crossed and recrossed by the trails of trappers. They opened the country to the southwest also, from Missouri to the Rio Grande. They reached the old Spanish settlement of Santa Fe.

Two famous trappers of this southwest country were Sylvester Pattie and his son James Ohio Pattie. Their adventures would fill a book. They explored the country of the Colorado and Gila rivers, gathering beaver skins. Hunted by Indians and starving, they wandered into Lower California and came from there to San Diego.

Governor Echeandia was uneasy. Only a little while before this, Jedediah Smith and his men had appeared in California. Were the Americans going to come in large numbers? He put the Patties in prison.

Sylvester Pattie was unable to endure any more. He died in prison. Young James Ohio was saved by a strange circumstance. Smallpox broke out among the mission Indians. Pattie

Families set forth for California

had a small amount of vaccine. The governor granted him his freedom if he would vaccinate the Californians. Pattie traveled through California vaccinating the Spanish and Indians by the thousand. Surely there were never so many aching arms in the land before. James Pattie remained some time in the country before he finally sailed away from Monterey.

Between 1830 and 1840 other men visited California. People in the States learned that it was possible to go to California without going by ship around the Horn. They pieced together the many stories they had heard of this warm, pleasant land. They became more and more interested. Men began to talk of going there with their families to make new homes.

They did not know the dangers ahead

The first party to carry out this purpose was led by a young man named John Bidwell. There were about seventy people in his party. Fifteen of them were women and children. They started from Sapling Grove in what is now eastern Kansas. With high hopes and happy plans they packed their wagons. They started northwest up the river valleys. Their guide was a priest who had been over the trail. Through the Rockies they made their way, into the part of the country we now call Wyoming. Here the priest went on to Oregon. Some of the people went with him. The rest clung to the idea of going to California.

They turned south to the Great Salt Lake. There they started across the dreary desert which Smith had crossed years before. They knew very little about the way. But they knew they must go west, not too far north and not too far south. It was a desolate country—a gray waste of rocks and sand. They had to travel slowly. Food became scarce. They suffered for lack of good water.

They neared the High Sierras. It was autumn and they shivered to think how hard it would be to cross them if snow should come. They left their wagons behind and packed their goods on horses and mules. They followed one stream after another, higher and higher. At last they came to one that flowed west. This encouraged them.

But the mountain gorges through which the stream ran were narrow and deep. They could scarcely find foothold. They were weak with hunger. Each day they thought they could go

126

no farther. They ate crows, wildcats, even coyotes, anything to keep life in their bodies.

At last they dragged themselves down into a beautiful valley. Could it be that they had reached California at last? They could not believe it, but it was true! The journey had taken them six months. It must have seemed much longer.

Bidwell's party was followed by others. Those who packed their furniture and food in covered wagons and set forth to California knew it was a long way. But they had no idea of the terrible things they would have to suffer. Some reached the desert in the blazing heat of summer. One after another died of thirst and heat. Some of the wagon trains were attacked by Indians. The High Sierras stood in the way like a wall, steep and rocky, deep with snow in winter. The wagons had to be left behind. Tired children were placed on the thin horses. The remaining food was carried on the backs of weary men. Animals died. Mothers starved, saving their food for their children. Whole families froze to death on the bleak heights.

But some kept themselves alive. Down out of the cruel mountains they came into the warm valleys of California. The first place they reached was Sutter's Fort on the Sacramento. How good it looked! Houses, cultivated fields, well-stored barns! The wilderness behind them! Genial John Sutter came to meet them, his hands stretched out in welcome. The starving were fed. The sick were cared for. It was like coming home.

Sutter gave them land. He hired the men to work for him. Whenever he heard of a group struggling through the mountains, he sent a rescue party with food to show them the way.

The Mexican officers of California were not at all pleased to see so many Americans coming over the mountains. The Americans would soon outnumber the Californians. They did not like it when Sutter welcomed them and gave them land.

Sutter's Fort

But this did not stop Captain Sutter. And he was not the only one who was kind to the newly arrived Americans. General Vallejo, a courteous Spanish gentleman, had a large *rancho* north of San Francisco Bay, not far from Sutter's land. He also welcomed the pioneers from the States.

Other Spanish people on the ranchos and in the pueblos were friendly. They did not mind the coming of the Americans. They were not happy under Mexican rule. So the thought of a possible change did not worry them.

128

✤✤✤✤✤✤✤✤✤✤✤✤✤✤✤✤✤✤✤✤✤✤✤✤✤✤✤✤✤✤✤✤✤✤✤✤✤✤✤

CHAPTER XIII

How Mexico Lost California

CALIFORNIA WAS an unhappy country under the government of Mexico. This was not strange. After the separation from Spain, the Mexicans could not keep peace in their own land. One revolution followed another. No leader stayed in power more than a few months. In such a state of affairs no one had time to think of California.

The soldiers at the presidios in California were not paid. They received no clothing or supplies. Ammunition ran low. The ports were not properly guarded. The only new settlers sent to California were lawbreakers out of the jails. Certainly these were not likely to make good citizens. The governors who were sent to Monterey had little interest in the welfare of California. They thought only of making themselves rich. They quarreled constantly with the captains of the presidios.

One reason for the lack of cooperation between Mexico and California was that it was so hard to reach one from the other. The sea voyage was rough and difficult. Mexican ships were scarce. The overland route was always a dangerous one because of deserts and unfriendly Indians.

Other countries were watching California. Not only the Boston Ships, but also English and French ships had traded in the California ports. They, too, had carried home stories of this rich and fertile land. It would be a prize for any nation.

England, France, and the United States all understood that things could not go on as they were. California would not remain under the Mexican flag. It would soon belong to another nation. Each wanted to be that nation. English, French, and American ships were in the Pacific Ocean ready to land at Monterey when the right moment came. English, French, and American agents were living in California, watching events, and sending reports home to their governments.

Thomas Larkin was an American merchant living at Monterey. In 1843 the government at Washington appointed him United States Consul to California. This meant that he was to help Americans living in California who needed assistance from their government, and that he was to look after the interests of the United States. Larkin was a wise man and could handle difficult matters with care and tact. Two years later James Knox Polk became President of the United States. He believed England wished to take California. He wrote to Thomas Larkin the Consul at Monterey:

"Do what you can very quietly to make the Californians friendly to the United States. Tell them we will not stir up trouble. But if they wish to free themselves from Mexico, the United States will protect them. Let them follow the example of Texas."

130

Nine years before this, Texas had freed herself from Mexico. As an independent republic, she had asked to be admitted to the United States. Congress had just voted to admit Texas as a state.

Thomas Larkin turned over his business to others and gave his whole time to this matter. He had many friends among the Spanish Californians. They talked freely with him. Some of them thought it would be wise to join the United States. One of these was General Vallejo, who had been a good friend of the American pioneers in California.

Of course, people from the United States who were living in California believed that California should belong to their country. Some of these Americans had lived in California many years. They had places of business in the pueblos or in the ports. They had married the beautiful daughters of the Spanish *rancheros*. They looked upon the Spanish Californians as relatives and friends, and had no wish to hurt them.

But the new settlers who were pouring through the mountains had different ideas. They did not understand the Spanish people. They did not trust nor like them. They believed the United States had a right to this country in which they were settling. The region in the north, around Sutter's Fort, was full of these new settlers. They knew little of the Spanish people or their laws.

Pio Pico was governor of California at this time. He had moved the capital from Monterey to Los Angeles. He spent most of his time quarreling with General José Castro, head

131

of the military forces at the presidio of Monterey. Each insisted that the other did not show him proper respect. Each demanded a larger share of the customs money from the port of Monterey than he was receiving. This was the only money the California officials had, as none came from Mexico.

These quarrels divided the feelings of the Spanish Californians. Some took the side of Pico; some followed Castro. Many were disgusted with both, and would take no part in public affairs.

If all had proceeded quietly, it is possible that Mr. Larkin's plan for a peaceful arrangement would have succeeded. California might have come into the United States without any fighting. But in such a restless and confused time it was hard to keep feelings peaceful and reasonable. People said hasty and thoughtless things. They were ready to take offense and willing to believe idle stories. They suspected those around them of plotting harm. It was a time when trouble could start all too readily.

About this time, over the mountains came Colonel John Frémont with a band of sixty men. They were explorers, engineers, and geologists belonging to the United States Army. They had been sent to find the best route to the Pacific Ocean. The California officials asked what United States soldiers were doing in their country without permission. Frémont replied that they were exploring. After collecting supplies they would march north to Oregon.

Instead of marching north, however, Frémont camped in

132

the Salinas valley, not far from Monterey. He was ordered to leave at once and to keep his men away from the port. He mounted a rugged hill called Gavilan Peak and prepared to resist General Castro, who was collecting soldiers in the valley. Suddenly, however, Frémont changed his plan, marched away by night and started up the Sacramento valley toward Oregon.

The actions of Frémont and his men made the Spanish Californians more uneasy than ever. Were the soldiers of the United States planning to capture the country? Rumors came of a dispute between the United States and Mexico over the boundaries of Texas. Would there be a war? How about all those American settlers in the Sacramento valley, with their long rifles and their odd way of talking? What were they going to do?

In the American settlements the whispers were even more excited and fearful. An army was on the way from Mexico! All the Americans were to be driven out of California into the mountains! General Castro was rounding up horses and getting ready to march on them!

They did not wait to find out if these things were true. They thought something must be done quickly, before the enemy could act. A group of men went out and captured some horses which were being sent to Castro. Frémont had returned from the north. They went to his camp to make their plans. Frémont did not say that he would join them. But no doubt it made them bolder to know that he was at hand with his trained soldiers.

133

One Sunday in June, 1846, thirty Americans marched to Sonoma and surrounded the home of General Vallejo. They told him they had come to take the town. They took the general and his brother prisoner and sent them to Frémont's camp, and from there to Sutter's Fort.

The Flag of the Bear Republic

They declared California a republic, free from Mexico. They chose William Ide as their captain. They made a flag for the new republic. It was white with a red stripe along the lower edge. On it were the words *California Republic*. They drew on it a star and a grizzly bear. The bear was an odd-looking animal. Somebody who wanted to be funny said that it looked like a pig. But up the flagpole fluttered the Bear Flag to wave over Sonoma.

134

At once many other Americans rushed to join the group at Sonoma. They were all very much in earnest about the new state. Frémont resigned from the United States Army and came to Sonoma with his soldiers. On the Fourth of July they had a celebration. Frémont became the leader of the Bear Republic.

Five days later word came that the United States was at war with Mexico. When two nations are at war each tries to capture part of the other's territory. It was for this that the ships had been waiting. Into the harbor of Monterey sailed an American ship with troops on board. There were no soldiers at the fort to resist them. Up went the Stars and Stripes to fly over the presidio of Monterey. The same thing happened at San Francisco, at San José, at Sutter's Fort.

At Sonoma the flag of the Grizzly Bear came down, and the flag of the United States of America waved on the pole where the Bear Flag had been. The brief days of the Bear Republic were over. It had lasted a little more than three weeks.

At first the Spanish Californians did not resist the troops of the United States. Commodore Stockton of the American Navy took charge of the situation. He sent Frémont with his men by ship to San Diego. He himself embarked for San Pedro to march to Los Angeles.

This news was enough for Governor Pico. He fled to his ranch near San Bernardino and from there to Lower California. General Castro had only one hundred men and no arms. He, too, gave up all thought of resistance. He got out of the country quickly, riding the Anza trail back to Sonora.

Frémont's men marched north from San Diego and joined Stockton's band coming from San Pedro. Together they entered Los Angeles and took possession. They raised the flag and declared California a territory of the United States. All seemed quiet and peaceful. Captain Gillespie with a force of fifty men was left in charge. Frémont and Stockton returned to Monterey. Kit Carson, the famous scout, one of Frémont's company, was sent to Washington with a report of what had been done.

Riding along the trail through Arizona, Kit met Captain Stephen W. Kearny, of the United States Army. He was in command of three hundred men, on his way to take possession of California. He became General Kearny a little later.

"No use to go on," said Kit Carson. "California is already conquered and at peace. Look here! I am carrying the news to Washington."

"I was ordered to California and I must go," said Kearny. "But I shall not need so many men." With that he sent two hundred men back toward Texas. He persuaded Kit Carson to turn about and guide him through the desert to California.

Meanwhile things had changed in California. Aroused by some of the younger men, the Spanish Californians were fighting for their country. They had chosen three leaders, José Maria Flores, José Antonio Carillo, and Andrés Pico, the brother of the fleeing governor.

136

The Spanish citizens of Los Angeles were in revolt against Captain Gillespie. With his men, Gillespie took a stand on a hill above the Plaza. He needed to get word to Stockton at Monterey. He chose one of his men, John Brown, to carry the message. Gillespie then fell back with his men to the harbor of San Pedro, hoping Stockton would send a ship with help.

"Lean John," as Brown was called, mounted a horse and set off. He rode like mad until his horse dropped under him. He tramped afoot for twenty-seven miles, got another horse and rode on. Wherever he could, he secured a fresh mount, never stopping for rest or sleep. When he reached Monterey, Stockton had left for San Francisco. On went "Lean John" for another long ride. He found Stockton and delivered his message. He had traveled five hundred miles in less than six days!

Stockton sent Captain Mervine at once by sea to San Pedro. Here Mervine found Gillespie and his men. The combined force, about three hundred men, started north toward the pueblo of Los Angeles. It was a hot autumn day. The way lay across a plain overgrown with wild mustard. In some places the dried stalks were six feet high. The sun blazed down on the marching men. Fine, hot dust filled their nostrils. Exhausted they made camp at the Dominguez rancho.

Next day their way was blocked by more than one hundred Spanish Californians under the command of José Carillo. The Californians had any and every kind of gun. They also carried home-made lances. These were willow poles tipped with files or knife blades. But they were mounted on fine horses—and they had a cannon!

The cannon was a little bronze four-pounder which had stood in the pueblo plaza. An old Mexican woman had hidden it when the Americans first approached the town. She brought it out for Carillo's men. They mounted it on the tongue and two wheels of a wagon, and yanked it about with lariats. They whisked the cannon up ahead of their forces, and used it first on one side and then on the other. They touched it off with lighted cigarettes.

The American soldiers tried to keep straight ahead. But the

The Americans reached the San Gabriel River

wretched little gun yapped at them from every side. They had no cannon. It was plainly useless to go on. They turned back to San Pedro with the gun barking at their heels. They reached the bay with four men killed and six wounded. This was called the Battle of Dominguez Ranch. It is sometimes called the Battle of Old Woman's Gun.

Led by Kit Carson, Kearny and his men were struggling through the desert. They reached California gaunt and weary from the heat and the long marches. Their horses were worn out. Stockton was at San Diego. He sent Gillespie with thirty-five men to meet Kearny. Before Kearny and Gillespie reached

Flores and his men were on a bluff beyond

San Diego, they met a company of well-mounted Californians under Andrés Pico. How they could ride, those Spanish *rancheros!* They pretended to retreat. The Americans came after them on their tired beasts, strung out in a long line. Suddenly the Californians wheeled and rode upon them! Their odd lances were ugly weapons in such hands. Sixteen or eighteen Americans were killed, and as many more were wounded before the Californians rode away. Among the wounded were General Kearny and Captain Gillespie.

In San Diego General Kearny and Commodore Stockton combined their forces. They led their troops from San Diego toward Los Angeles. It was cold. The men were badly clothed, the horses poor and weak. At the crossing of the San Gabriel River they met the Californians again, under Flores. The river was wide and bordered by quicksand. Flores and his men had two cannon on a bluff beyond. It was a bad outlook. Somehow, Kearny's men dragged their guns and baggage wagons across the stream and up the hill. There was a sharp clash, and suddenly it was over. The Californians left the bluff and by the next morning they were gone.

Flores made one more stand against the Americans, beside the Los Angeles River. Then he drew off his little band of hard-riding rancheros. He probably thought their cause was hopeless. The Americans were too many for them. Again the Stars and Stripes waved over Los Angeles.

Frémont's forces were marching down from Monterey. General Flores left the country and went to Sonora. Andrés Pico was left in command of the Californians. It was Frémont and Pico who signed the treaty at the old Cahuenga ranch house, in January, 1847. California's part of the war was over.

One year later, in February, 1848, the United States made peace with Mexico. The two countries signed a treaty. By this treaty the United States paid Mexico the sum of $15,000,000. Mexico gave up her claim to all land north of the Rio Grande, and from there across to the Pacific Ocean, south of San Diego.

This meant that California belonged to the United States. With it came the great stretch of country between California and Texas. Later this country would form the states of Arizona, New Mexico, Nevada, Utah, and Colorado.

The Gold Rush

CHAPTER XIV

****

Gold in the Mountains

IN JANUARY, 1848, the Mexican and American generals made the treaty which gave California to the United States. While this was going on, a very surprising thing was happening at Sutter's Fort.

Captain John Sutter had decided that he needed another sawmill. He chose as the builder of the mill a quiet hard-working man named James Marshall. Marshall took some men with him and found a good place for a mill. It was forty-five miles above the fort on the American River. There were plenty of pine trees there to be sawed into lumber. He went to work building the mill. It was soon nearly ready for the wheel and the machinery.

A channel or ditch had to be dug from the river past the mill and back to the river again. This was needed in order that water from the river might run through the ditch. This water would run under the mill wheel and turn the wheel. Such a channel is called a "millrace." A gate called a "head gate" shut off the water when it was not needed.

A millrace is in two parts, the headrace and the tailrace.

145

The tailrace is the part of the ditch in which the water leaves the mill. When Marshall and his men had dug the tailrace, he let water run through it overnight. He wanted to wash away the loose dirt and deepen the ditch.

On the 24th of January, after Marshall had closed the head gates, he stood looking down at the rocks and sand in the tailrace as the water ran off. What were those shiny bits? He gathered them up and looked at them closely. Could they be grains of gold?

He took the stuff to his room and pounded it with a hammer. It did not break and crumble. It bent and flattened out, as pure gold does. He wrapped it up carefully and took it down to the fort. Together he and Sutter examined it again. They weighed it. Its weight was right for gold. They tested it in every way they could. It met every test. Gold it was! Pure gold! Out of the bed of the American River.

They went back to the mill and looked about on all sides. They found more grains of gold. Everywhere were traces of the yellow metal. Sutter thought of his fields.

"Don't tell the men," he said. "If they know there is gold about here, I'll get no more work out of them. My mill will not be finished, nor my wheat harvested. Every man will leave his work to look for gold."

But such a secret as this could not be kept long. Others learned of it. The news spread to Monterey and San Francisco.

At first people did not believe the story. They paid little attention. A few were curious and went to see for themselves.

146

They came back with little sacks of gold dust, each worth a goodly sum of money. Excitement rose. By spring everyone in California who could was going to the mines.

They left their houses and shops. The towns were almost empty. All the men who could buy or borrow tools packed up what food they had and started. They were off to hunt their fortunes in the mountains and along the streams. There were not enough people left to sell food and tools to those who wanted them. Food and tools became very scarce.

From the ports ships took the story back to the States and all over the world. What a story it was! California, the land of sunshine and beauty, was now a land of riches! The tales grew more amazing. The rivers were full of gold! The mountains were yellow with gold! Anybody could dig up bushels of it! A man could be rich in a few days!

Everyone wanted to go immediately to California. Those who could leave their homes began to get ready. The papers printed lists of things needed for the trip or at the mines. Such a buying and packing as there was!

It was a long journey from the eastern part of the United States to California, no matter how a man chose to go. It was a journey beset with hardships. The people in the center of the country loaded up their wagons and ox teams and started west along the pioneer trails. Those who lived on the eastern coast preferred to go by ship, down around the Horn and up through the Pacific. The ships were crowded with men bound for California. There were not enough ships to take those who wanted to go. Anything that would sail was loaded and started off, whether it was fit for such a trip or not.

Some people went by ship as far as the Isthmus of Panama. Then they traveled by canoe and on muleback, or afoot over the rough trails to the shore of the Pacific. Here they waited their chance to board a ship going up the coast to California. There were not enough ships here either. It cost a great deal of money for passage in one of them. Men paid a thousand dollars for a chance to sleep in a corner of the deck or on a coil of rope in a ship bound for California.

When San Francisco Bay was reached it was easy to see where all the ships were. The harbor was full of deserted ships,

Some miners worked along the streams

rocking at anchor. Their crews had left them and rushed off to the mines.

Marshall found the first gold in January of 1848. It took months for the news to travel, and more months for people to reach California. It was 1849 before the great rush came. The throngs of people who hurried into California after gold are often called the Forty-Niners. Thousands of them reached Sutter's Fort and, from there, followed the trails into the mountains to look for gold.

Some of them worked along the streams, sifting the sand for golden grains, digging nuggets out of cracks in the rocks. Some went farther back, dug up the soil and brought it to

Some dug into the sides of the hills

the water. They used cradles for washing out the gold. A cradle was a long box on rockers, open at one end. The dirt full of gold specks was put into it. Water was turned in and the box was rocked. The heavy flakes of gold sank to the bottom of the cradle and stayed there. The water and dirt ran out at the open end.

The gold that was easy to find was soon gone. Then men had to go farther. They had to tunnel into the sides of the hills or dig deep into the stream beds. Still gold seekers came by the thousand. They came from every country on earth.

They built little cabins to live in. Wherever someone had found a good "digging" for gold, a town of little cabins grew up like magic. When the gold was gone from that place, the men left their huts and moved on to a new location. Many such little towns were left vacant. Some of them are still to be seen today, little ghost towns made up of ruins that once were houses.

While this was going on, San Francisco grew into a big city. It was not a beautiful city. There was no time to make buildings beautiful. The streets were not paved. The mud was sometimes so deep that wagons and horses sank into it until they were buried.

It was a noisy, crowded city. There were many gambling places and drinking shops. Men came back from the mines with bags full of gold dust. They wanted to spend money. They wanted to buy good meals. But it was easier to find men with bags of gold than good food. Everything cost a great deal.

Eggs were a dollar apiece, milk was fifty cents a quart, onions were a dollar a pound, and brown sugar was three dollars a pound. Other things were just as costly.

Of course, there were bad men, too lazy to hunt for their own gold. They stayed in the cities and gambled with the miners to get their gold away from them. Many men found a fortune in gold dust only to lose it to gamblers or have it stolen. Sometimes they went back to look for more. Some men found and lost more than one fortune. Others took their gold dust back to the States, and sold it for enough to live on in comfort all their lives.

There were men who were clever enough to notice that cities were growing up overnight. They saw here a chance to buy and sell land or to put up buildings for sale or for rent. They made large fortunes in the leaping growth of California land values.

There were miners who had no luck at all. They did not find enough gold to make them rich, not even enough to pay them for hunting. Some of these drifted about, mining a little here and a little there. They spent their lives thinking they were just about to locate the best claim of all, but never quite succeeding.

Some of the unlucky miners were wiser. They stopped wasting their time digging in the hills. Like the clever city men, they saw an opportunity in the growth of a new region. They went to work as farmers, raising food for the miners or grain for the market. They found out that California was a

151

wonderful country for fruit-growing and planted orchards. This was another way, and a very good way, of seeking a fortune.

Since many people made large fortunes in the gold fields or elsewhere, it is sad to think that Captain Sutter and James Marshall both died poor. Captain Sutter quarreled with various people about his rights and, because of many lawsuits, lost most of his property. Marshall, too, was unfortunate. When he died, a poor man, in 1885, almost everyone had forgotten that it was he who first found gold at Sutter's mill. Since that time, however, a statue has been erected in his honor. It stands on a hill overlooking the spot where, in 1848, he first saw the glitter of metal in the millrace.

++

California Becomes a State

THE YEAR 1849 was a very unsettled and confusing time for the people of California. One cause was the excitement of the gold rush. Another was the lack of a regular system of law and government. This would have been bad enough in quiet, orderly times. But with thousands of men from all over the world rushing into California to look for gold it was very bad indeed.

By the treaty with Mexico, California had been made a part of the United States. But she was not yet a state. There was no satisfactory plan for making or enforcing laws. There were no men to act as governors but those generals of the United States Army who were stationed in California. Everyone expected the Congress of the United States to make California a state, or at least a territory. Everyone thought laws would be provided and a governor elected.

Instead of taking care of these matters, Congress was quarreling. The Congressmen from the southern states said that California must be a slave state. Those from the northern

153

states insisted that she must be a free state. They ended by refusing to make her a state at all.

When Congress finished its session and went home without doing anything for them, the people of California were greatly disappointed. "We *must* have laws," they said, "and men to see that the laws are obeyed."

They did have the old Mexican laws. But these were of little use. They were laws for a quiet rural land of missions and ranches, with a few small towns. In fact, the Mexican laws were merely the instructions Bucareli had given long ago to Rivera and the rules Governor Neve had made for his pueblos. They were not enough for these thousands of people from different countries, people used to different ways of living. The country had changed too suddenly. The old laws would not do.

In some of the towns people took things into their own hands. They made laws and chose officials. But this could not be done in all places. Then, too, it was most confusing not to have the same system through all the country.

In the noisy little mining camps dishonest men stole other men's gold. Men were killed in fights. The miners made laws of their own, and they made short work of lawbreakers. But as a whole conditions were very bad indeed. Good earnest citizens were much troubled.

General Riley, who was acting governor at the time, decided to hold a meeting or convention. He asked each town to choose men to come to the convention. These men would

154

decide on a plan or set of rules for the governing of California. Such a plan is called a constitution.

This was done. Forty-eight men, chosen from all parts of California, gathered at Monterey in September, 1849. They were a group of strong, able citizens. Some of whom we have heard were there—Thomas Larkin, the former consul, Captain John Sutter, courtly General Vallejo, and other good American and Spanish citizens. And there were younger men who had come recently with the gold seekers—lawyers, merchants, soldiers. They were all very much in earnest.

One of the first things they did was to vote that California should be a free state and not a slave state. So that question was settled for Congress. They fixed the boundaries of the state just as they are today. They ordered the starting of public schools. They drew up a set of laws for taxation and for the election of public officials.

The first election was held the following month. The people voted to accept the new constitution. They elected their governor and two representatives. These two representatives and two chosen Senators set out for Washington to see to it that California was made a state.

This was no easy task. First they had to bring a bill before Congress. (A proposed law, before it has been passed by Congress, is called a bill.) After the bill was brought in, they had to persuade the Congressmen to vote for it. The North and the South were still quarreling hotly about slave states and free states.

Month after month the debate about California went on. Some of our greatest statesmen took part in it. At the very end of the following summer the bill was voted on and passed. President Fillmore signed it on the ninth of September, 1850. This made it a law. California became a state—the thirty-first state admitted to the Union.

In California people waited anxiously for news from Washington. So many months passed that it seemed as if the news would never come. One October day a ship sailed through the Golden Gate into San Francisco Bay, with guns booming, flags and streamers fluttering. Crowds rushed to the dock.

"News from Washington!" shouted one to another.

The news had come at last. California was admitted to the Union! Everybody was wild with joy. They threw their hats in the air. They rang bells and fired guns. Fireworks lit up the shores of the bay. There was a parade and great merry-making.

Word went out to other towns. Men on horseback galloped in different directions to spread the news. Stagecoach drivers whipped up their horses. In every village people came running to hear, "California is admitted to the Union!"

The shout went across the land, to little mining camps in the hills, to quiet pueblos in the south, to distant ports and ranches. The people were full of a great joy. They were encouraged to make plans. With the United States to help California, her future was bright.

California was now a state with well-planned laws and with
156

officials to see that the laws were carried out. But the city of San Francisco still had a great deal of trouble because of the dishonest and wicked people who had come there after the gold rush.

Things became so bad that, in 1851, two hundred of the best citizens formed a Vigilance Committee. The work of this committee was to drive criminals out of the city and help in other ways to see that the laws were enforced.

The committee worked hard. Many dishonest people were turned over to the police or sent out of town. Several murderers were executed. Conditions in San Francisco were very much improved. After a time the Vigilance Committee of 1851 was disbanded. ·

But after a few years the gambling and stealing and killing began again. So another Vigilance Committee was formed in 1856, and again San Francisco was given a cleaning up. The Committee did its work well, and after it disbanded no other Vigilance Committee had to be started for many years. The city officials had learned to do their work without such help. However, on July 23, 1877, general lawlessness and Chinese riots led to a revival of the Vigilance Committee and the enlistment of 6000 citizens.

✤✤

How the West Was Tied to the East

CAPTAIN SHALER had said that California should belong to a nation which would help her make the most of her riches. He was right. A good start had been made. California was now one of the United States. She had good laws. She had a governor and other state officers. She had representatives and Senators to look after her interests in Washington.

But one very important thing needed to be done before California would be a real part of the mother country. There remained the great problem of distance. This must be overcome in some way.

California was too far away from the rest of the United States. It took three months to travel from St. Louis to San Francisco in a covered wagon. It took five or six months, often more, to sail around the Horn. The quickest possible way to travel or to send messages was by ship to the Isthmus of Panama, across the Isthmus, and by ship again up the coast. Even with good luck this took five weeks.

The mail ships were likely to go directly to San Francisco. Mail for southern California was, therefore, often very much delayed. Letters from New York sometimes took seven or eight months to reach Los Angeles.

People felt that some way must be found to send letters and important news more quickly. During the first ten years after California came into the Union a number of ways were tried. The swiftest carriers proved to be the Overland Mail and the Pony Express.

The Overland Mail

The Overland Mail was started first. It was a stagecoach route between San Francisco and St. Louis. On its way east, it passed through Los Angeles, then east and south into Arizona by the old pioneer roads and trade routes, and in a rough semicircle up to Tipton, a point not far from St. Louis. The railway from the East ended at Tipton.

The coach carried the mailbags and six or eight passengers. It was pulled by from four to six horses or mules, which were

159

changed at stations along the way. The animals were driven at a steady pace. The coach was supposed to make the journey one way in twenty-five days. But the trip was usually made in shorter time. Later, a route was laid out farther north, over which the coach could travel in seventeen to twenty days.

It was not a comfortable way for passengers to travel, cramped into a small space for so many days. The only chances to stretch were at the way-stations where horses were changed. Passengers had to carry along their own food, for there was little to be had on the road.

It was an exciting way to travel. There was ever the possibility of danger. The coach might have to ford a stream swelled by floods. It might be attacked by Indians. It might be held up by bandits. But, even so, most people thought it much better than a long uncomfortable sea voyage.

Those in the northern part of California were not satisfied with the route of the Overland Mail. The eastern news reached Los Angeles several days ahead of San Francisco. People felt that there should be a way to send mail across the mountains farther north. So the Pony Express was planned, and the first Pony Express mail went through in April, 1860.

The Pony Express route started in San Francisco and went to Sacramento, the thriving city which had grown up around Sutter's Fort. From there the Pony Express entered the foothills and crossed the high mountains by the winding passes of the old Sierra trails, to Nevada, to Utah, and on to St. Joseph, Missouri.

160

The riders of the Pony Express were strong young men, who could ride like the wind and who were afraid of nothing. They wore buckskin clothes with the hair outside to shed the rain. They could not stop for storms. Thrust into their belts were pistols and sharp knives, because they might encounter

The Pony Express

savage Indians. Their business was to get the mailbags across without turning aside for anything.

Each Pony Express rider rode one hundred miles, changing horses every twenty-five miles. If something prevented the next rider from taking his place, he had to ride farther. After the rider had rested, he rode back to carry mail the other way.

The mailbags, passed along from one rider to the other, made the trip from San Francisco to Missouri in nine or ten days. This was wonderful speed! How astonished people would have been, to know that seventy-five years later an airplane would carry mail from ocean to ocean in seventeen hours!

There were some famous riders of the Pony Express. One of the best known of these was "Buffalo Bill" Cody. But, in spite of brave riders and fine horses, the Pony Express lasted less than two years. It was found to be very costly. It was impossible to keep the trips regular in winter when snow filled the mountain passes. Most important of all, there was suddenly less need for this method of sending messages. A telegraph line was completed from Omaha to San Francisco and Los Angeles.

The telegraph was the first thing that tied the West closely to the East. Now the country's news, and important personal messages, could go quickly. But travel for passengers was still very slow. For years there had been talk of building a railroad to California. But many people laughed at the idea. What? Lay ties and rails across those endless miles of burning desert and over those steep mountains? Impossible!

It would, indeed, be a huge undertaking. It would cost great sums of money. However, the Government sent out bands of engineers to look into the matter, and to map out possible routes across the country. Then a dispute arose over which route was best. Some wanted the railroad in the north, some in the south, some in the middle.

A certain young engineer was at work on a small railroad line in California. He looked often at the High Sierras. There must be a place where a railroad could go through. He rode his horse over the trails, surveying here and there. He tried

162

to find the best route for a railroad. This young man was Theodore Judah.

Young Judah talked about his plan to everyone who would listen. One day he found four men who would do more than listen. They grew interested in his idea. All four were merchants owning stores in Sacramento. They were men of good sense and determination. Now they made up their minds to build a railroad. Their names were Leland Stanford, Collis P. Huntington, Mark Hopkins, and Charles Crocker. Later they were called the "Big Four."

The first thing needed was to get the government of the United States to help with land and money. Huntington and Judah went to Washington. They drew up a bill on which Congress could vote. Perhaps you think everyone was in favor of the railroad. No, indeed. There were still many who thought the whole idea foolish. They believed that to try such a railroad would be a great waste of time and money.

The Civil War had begun. California was a free state, and her soldiers went east to fight with the northern forces. How far away California seemed! It was plainly necessary that somehow people should be able to travel across the country more quickly. After much debate Congress passed the bill. President Lincoln signed it, making it a law. But young Judah died. The work had to go on without the man who had first dreamed of it.

Stanford and Hopkins took care of the California end. Money was raised and legal papers prepared. One thing after

163

another happened to block the four partners. They spent time, effort, and money; they risked all they had in the venture. Crocker was put in charge of constructing the road itself. He hired engineers to make the plans and workmen to carry them out. He bought steel and lumber.

The plan was to build two railroads. The Union Pacific would start at Omaha and build a track west. The Central Pacific would start at Sacramento and build a track up over the mountains and down again. This track would go east until the two tracks met. The part from west to east was Crocker's railroad. You can see that he had a real job ahead of him.

The tracks met in northern Utah

Each road had the best of it in some ways and the worst of it in other ways. Crocker had to build his track through steep, narrow, winding mountain passes. But he had plenty of trees growing right beside the track for timber. He used them for ties, for trestles to support bridges, and for sheds to shelter the work from winter snows. The other railroad crossed flat country. But the timber had to be hauled a long way. There was endless trouble because of Indian raids.

Both roads had difficulty getting laborers. The Civil War was still going on when the work was begun. Most of the men who could have worked were fighting. Because of the

There was a great celebration

war, too, both roads had trouble getting steel and other materials. But somehow the work went steadily on.

The track through the mountains was finished. After that, Crocker's men could work faster. He brought thousands of Chinese to this country. He trained them like soldiers, and they made fine workmen. The two railroads began a race. Which could lay more miles of track before they met? It was very exciting. Never had track been laid so fast. One day Crocker's men put down more than ten miles of track. That was the world's record.

The two tracks met in northern Utah. They were joined on May 10, 1869, and there was a great celebration. California sent a piece of laurel wood for the last tie, and a spike of pure gold to be driven into it. The presidents of the two roads took turns pounding the spike into place with a silver sledge hammer. Telegraph wires had been fastened to it. Every blow of the silver hammer made bells ring in far distant cities.

The people of California were beside themselves with joy. Every town rang its bells. Locomotive whistles shrieked wildly. The West was truly tied to the East. People could now go from the Atlantic coast to the Pacific in seven or eight days instead of in long weary weeks or months. This happened, as has been said, in the spring of 1869. Just one hundred years had passed since Governor Portolá and Father Serra reached San Diego and started the first settlement in California.

How California Grew

CHAPTER XVII

❖❖

Changes in California

EVER SINCE the white men came, changes had been taking place in California. These changes mark the history of California into divisions. From the ringing of Father Serra's first mission bells in 1769 to the ringing of the bells which announced the joining of the railroads in 1869 was just one hundred years. This century divides into three parts.

The first fifty years were the years of the golden Spanish period. This was a time of slow and gradual change. Many people had a share in it, friars and soldiers and settlers; Captain Pérez sailing back and forth in the good ship *San Antonio,* Lieutenant Ayala in the *San Carlos* exploring San Francisco Bay, Anza leading the way across the desert. Together they turned the wild country of the Indians into a peaceful, rural Spanish land.

The next thirty years were the troubled years of Mexican rule. There was growing discontent among the people and quarreling among those who governed. The missions were secularized. Their buildings fell into ruins. Their gardens and vineyards withered away. Their great herds of cattle

169

passed into the hands of wealthy rancheros. The Indians were vanishing. Americans from the United States were coming over the mountains into California. And, finally, the Mexican War gave California to the United States.

The last twenty years were the interval years between Mexican California and American California. They were years of rapid changes, changes which were not all pleasant or just. Gold was discovered. Suddenly, from all over the world came the gold seekers. Towns in the north sprang up and became cities—San Francisco, Sacramento, Stockton. California became a state of the Union. Her government was made American in form. But California was not yet a truly American state like her sisters in the Union. The United States was still too far away to give her the help she needed.

During these years the busy new life of California centered in the northern part, around the Bay and the great rivers. Here the Forty-Niners had settled. Here the railroad was being pushed through the mountains.

In the south there were fewer changes. Los Angeles was still a sleepy pueblo. On the sloping plains about her, herds of cattle grazed lazily. The northern people called her the Queen of the Cow Counties. The mission settlements and ports of the south coast were too far from the gold mines to feel the stir.

Some of the new settlers, however, began to drift south. The fertile lands of the central valley and the southern plains attracted them. They wished to own and plant this California

170

land. At once there arose the question of the land titles.

Most of the land in central and southern California was owned by *rancheros*. Even the mission domains had been given by the Mexican governors to their friends for ranches. These ranches were very large. In a land of little rain a ranch needs to be large to provide enough grass for a herd of cattle. The ranch owners had so much land that they did not care about the exact boundaries. Often a man did not know where his land stopped and his neighbor's began. It made little difference, for the herds ran together. They were separated only once or twice a year, at branding time.

This was all very well when the land was owned by a few men and used for raising cattle, but a change had come. The new settlers had other purposes. Some wanted to raise wheat. Some wished to plant fruit trees or grapevines. When they bought land they had to know how many acres they were buying. They had to be very sure who owned it. If they did not pay the right owner there would be a dispute about it later.

In 1851 the United States Government appointed a group of men called a Land Commission. The Spanish ranch owners were told to come before this commission and prove what land belonged to them. This was called "clearing their titles." Many of them could not clear their titles. Perhaps the papers containing the record were lost. Perhaps the rocks or trees which had marked the boundaries had disappeared. There were many such difficulties.

171

The men chosen by our Government to decide these things did their best. But the land laws had been made by men who did not understand conditions in California. These laws were not always clear or just. Dishonest lawyers, money-lenders, and business men took advantage of this fact in order to make themselves rich. Some of the *rancheros* who had once been wealthy spent so much money paying lawyers to help them that they became poor. Others lost all they had, for lack of proof, and went away to Mexico. The United States lost many men who would have made good citizens. This is a sad page of California's history.

A little later another thing happened to discourage cattle-raising. The winter of 1863–64 was very dry. No rain fell and no grass grew on the hills. The cattle on the ranches died by thousands. These cattle were the wealth of the ranches. When they died of starvation the *rancheros* had no money to pay their taxes. Their lands had to be sold. Many of them had nothing left. Others had so little that they gave up their remaining land and their homes and then they went to Mexico.

Ranch land sold very cheaply. At one time it could be bought for a dollar and a half an acre. Some land was sold for as little as fifty cents an acre.

Much of this ranch land was bought by arriving settlers for wheat farms. For a few years wheat was the biggest crop in California. It was excellent wheat, so hard and dry that it could be shipped long distances without spoiling. Sheep

172

raising, also, got a good start at this time. Sheep can graze in rough country, and they need very little shelter.

These were some of the changes which were taking place in California during the twenty years after the discovery of gold. During these years the Civil War was being fought in the East. Stagecoaches were plying back and forth between California and Missouri. And Crocker and his laborers were laying the ties of the Central Pacific Railroad.

With the completion of the railroad a new era began for California. People came from the eastern part of the United States in increasing numbers. Scores of towns and villages appeared and grew vigorously. Still the greatest activity was in the north. But the turn of the south was coming. The Union Pacific Railroad proved so successful that other railroad companies were interested. Sixteen years later two other roads extended their rails across the continent to California, the Southern Pacific and the Santa Fe. These railroads opened the doors of southern California to the East.

In 1886 the three railroads entered a race to see which could sell the most tickets to California. Each road owned land in California which was for sale. They wished people to come and settle in the new state. Railroad tickets from points along the Mississippi River to California, which had cost one hundred and twenty-five dollars, grew cheaper and cheaper until they sold for five dollars each. For one day the fare from Missouri to Los Angeles was *one dollar*. Such cheap fares brought great numbers of people to live in California.

173

And so it was that with the building of the railroads other changes began in California, truly American changes. Things were done which took the imagination, the courage, and the energy that belong to the American people. Gradually conditions that were unsatisfactory were improved or corrected. The story of the last seventy years in California is a story of hard problems solved and rich rewards won.

CHAPTER XVIII

Black Riches

CALIFORNIA HAD other wealth than gold and fruit and grain. Something was to be found there that was more important than all the gold that brought the Forty-Niners. This was oil, or petroleum.

There were spots in California where the ground was oily. It had always been so. The earth was so full of oil at these places that it formed a sort of pitch or asphalt. The Indians had long known these spots. They used the pitch to calk the holes and seams of their boats. They spread it over their roofs to keep out the rain. The men fastened their bone fishhooks to their fiber lines with it. The women used it to stick the basket hoppers on the grinding stones.

In 1769 Governor Portolá and Father Crespí had camped beside the Spring of the Alders of San Estevan. Father Crespí wrote in his diary of the strange boiling marshes near by, where water ran to one side and oil to the other. The Spanish called the oily earth *brea.* A little later the settlers of Los Angeles used it to roof their houses.

Many years later Governor Pico gave his brother Andrés

part of the lands of the Mission San Fernando. In one of the canyons on this ranch, Andrés Pico found an oily place. He and his nephew dug shallow trenches in the hillside and let them fill with oil. This thick dirty oil they used in some experiments. Andrés Pico is sometimes called California's first oil man. This was about the time that gold was discovered. But no one thought then that oil, too, would mean riches to California.

In 1859, ten years after the gold rush, the first oil well in the United States was sunk. This was the Drake well in Pennsylvania. There was much excitement about it. A great interest

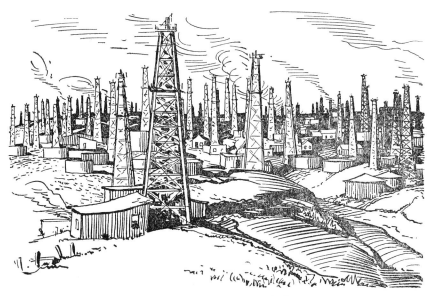

Derricks topped the hills

in oil sprang up in California. Everyone wished to own or rent oil land. Pico Canyon was sold, and the other well-known oily spots. Wells were dug, or tunnels cut into the hillsides.

Seeking for oil was not like seeking for gold. A man could not work alone. Digging wells with shovels was not satisfactory. After the railroads were built, machinery was brought to California and wells were drilled. Pipes were put down into the ground to bring up the oil. This cost money. Men who could not afford to buy such machinery alone formed groups and worked together. Each paid a share of the expense and received a share of the oil produced

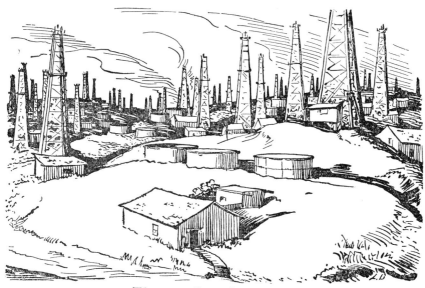

They swallowed up towns

The thick black oil as it came from the earth was called "crude oil." It was piped into a factory called a "refinery," to be cleaned. By heating, it could be separated into different grades of oil. In the early days oil was used in lamps for lighting, in stoves for fuel, and for oiling machinery. As the years passed, new uses were found for it.

In 1900 it was proved that oil could be used as fuel for locomotive engines. That was an important discovery for California. Coal was expensive. It had to be brought all the way from the East. Oil could be obtained in the state. It was cheaper than coal. It was cleaner. Then came automobiles. The whole world was soon riding in motor cars. These motors used gasoline. Gasoline was made from oil. If good for running locomotives, and automobiles, why not for running ships? This idea startled the world. Other countries began to buy oil from California. More oil was sold. More riches poured into California in return for her oil.

The tall frame to support the machine for drilling an oil well is called a "derrick." As more wells were drilled more derricks appeared. They stood close together like a strange kind of forest. Such forests sprang up in the San Joaquin valley, along the coast near Santa Barbara, and around Los Angeles. They topped the hills overlooking the harbor of San Pedro, they fringed the beaches, they stood along the old mission road, they dotted the state. Gardens disappeared where the derricks came. Growing towns were swallowed up.

178

Houses were torn down to make way for the pumping wells
For the finding of oil meant riches.

Deeper and deeper wells were drilled. Five thousand, eight
thousand, ten thousand feet, nearly two miles down into the
earth. The little Drake well of 1859, only seventy feet deep,
was a toy beside these wells. In the San Joaquin valley lay a
stretch of wrinkled brown hills, barren and ugly. Far down
under these hills was found a most amazing store of oil. "The
Sleeping Giant of Kettleman Hills" they called it. It was a
a giant of power waiting for men to set it to work turning
wheels.

Great pipe lines spread like a net across the state. They
carried oil from the fields to the refineries. They carried oil
to the harbors where tanker ships waited to take it across the
ocean.

This giant oil business brought a new problem to southern
California. The old port of San Pedro had never been a good
harbor. It was very shallow. Ships had to anchor out from
shore a long way. Their cargoes had to come to land in small
boats.

The government of the United States had already improved
the harbor by dredging it deeper. But people said more must
be done. The channels must be deepened still further and a
breakwater must be built. Los Angeles needed a real harbor.
Not only the oil trade demanded this, but also the trade in
oranges. For southern California had become a great center
for raising citrus fruits—oranges, lemons, and grapefruit.

179

A great harbor could not be built without government help. At first it seemed impossible to get this help. People laughed at the idea as they had laughed, years before, at the idea of a railroad. "Why should the Government spend money on such a harbor?" they asked. "It's not a harbor at all; it's nothing but a mud flat!"

But the citizens of Los Angeles would not give up. The

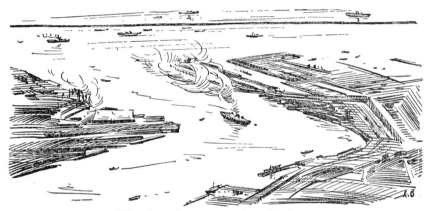

The breakwater at San Pedro

fruit and oil of southern California had to be sent to San Francisco Harbor by rail. This caused a waste of time and money. A harbor was needed in the south.

At last the battle was won. The Government granted the improved harbor to Los Angeles, and agreed to assist with the work and expense. There was a good deal of delay after the bill was passed—delay which the citizens of Los Angeles found very trying. But work was finally begun in 1898. This was in one of the years when William McKinley was President.

The harbor shores became a part of the city of Los Angeles. A breakwater more than two miles long was built. It was like a long arm flung out into the ocean to form a curving bay, where ships could be sheltered from wind and waves. Channels were dredged deeper. Docks and piers were constructed.

Great ocean liners and freighters came safely into the new harbor. They came from all the countries on the globe. They brought to southern California cargoes of all kinds, among them many strange things. Carpets and sauces came from India; nuts, cocoa beans, and coffee from Brazil; spices and woven grass baskets from Africa. And out of the harbor of Los Angeles went ships heavily laden with the golden fruits of California and huge tankers full of California oil.

++

CHAPTER XIX

The Problem of Water

NEW SETTLERS found California quite different from the eastern states. There it was cold in winter and warm in summer. The climate of the south was much warmer than that of the north. In California things were not divided in this way. Temperatures were more even. There was a great variety of climate, but the mountains and the ocean had more to do with causing cold and heat than winter and summer, or location north or south.

In the East, rain might fall at any time during the year— enough rain to water growing things. In most of California rain fell only in the winter months, from November to May. Parts of California did not have much rainfall even then. Some places had almost none at all. But even the desert places made fertile gardens if water could be supplied.

Water was the great need in California. Securing a supply of water for the whole year was the greatest problem the new settlers had to meet. They soon learned that it was useless to build a home and plant an orchard or garden unless they were sure of such a supply. For this reason the story of the

182

last seventy years in California is largely the story of this problem of water supply.

There were two parts to the water problem. Two things had to be done, in order that fruit and vegetables would grow. First, the rain that fell in winter must be stored for use in summer. Second, water must be brought from the places that had plenty to those that had little or none.

The region of greatest rainfall is the range of high mountains called the Sierra Nevada. These mountains extend down the state from north to south. Their tops are covered with snow for much of the year. Rain and melting snow form streams which flow down the western slopes into two great rivers. From the north comes the Sacramento, from the south the San Joaquin. Together they empty into the Bay of San Francisco. The people who settled in this long river valley brought water from the rivers in pipes and ditches to irrigate their fields and orchards in the dry season.

In the southern part of the state the problem was greater. Here the mountains are lower and there is less rain. Winter rains cause the streams to flow. But this water runs quickly away to the sea or sinks down under the ground. In summer the stream beds are dry. Below the sandy top soil of many of these southern valleys is a layer of hard rock. The water that sinks into the ground is held in this rock basin. The settlers in the south dig wells to reach the underground basins. In winter they turn the flowing streams into their irrigation ditches. In summer they pump water from the underground supply for their trees and gardens.

In order to keep the precious water from running away to the sea, the people of California built dams in the mountains. By putting a wall of rock or concrete across a mountain stream, they held back the water in a lake called a "reservoir." When water was needed, gates were opened, and the water flowed down into the ditches. When heavy rains filled the reservoirs, water was let out onto the wide sandy stream beds called "washes." Here it sank down to fill up the underground basins and supply the wells. In this way the farmers secured a supply of water for use whenever it was needed.

These things were not done all at once. They were a part of the steady changes which made California a garden state. At first each man built his own little dam, with ditches to carry the water to his land. Here and there neighbors banded together and built a larger dam. Every growing town had its own water problem. The faster the town grew the greater that problem was. The dam must be strong enough to hold back the heavy rains and keep them from flooding the town. The reservoir must be large enough to hold water for an increasing population.

Often there was trouble about the right to use the water in a stream. If a group near the mountains built a dam to hold their water supply, those who lived lower down on the stream cried out that their water had been stolen. They believed that they had a right to the water they needed. These quarrels

184

sometimes grew quite fierce, causing bloodshed. Water was so important that it meant ruin or success.

Laws were made, telling exactly what were the rights of all the people living near a stream to the use of the water. These rights were called "riparian rights." It was not easy to make such laws. After they were passed, judges and lawyers argued over their meaning. Even today California cities very often get into disputes over riparian rights, and much money and time are spent getting these disputes settled.

Books of stories could be written about the settlers who came to California and their struggles to get started. Railroad officials advertised California land, and made tempting offers. Sometimes a number of families in an eastern state formed a colony. They bought a large piece of land and came to California together. One of the first groups to do this came out in 1870 and founded the town of Riverside in Southern California. They planned to raise oranges. When they arrived and saw the land they had bought they were greatly disappointed. The nearest water was the Santa Ana River, nine miles away. They had paid for their land. They *must* have water. There was only one thing to do. They set to work with courage and determination and dug an irrigation canal from the river to their land. This took months, but it was finally finished. Then they were able to plant the seeds for their groves of young orange trees.

Two years later one of these colonists Mrs. Eliza Tibbets received two small orange trees of a new kind from the De-

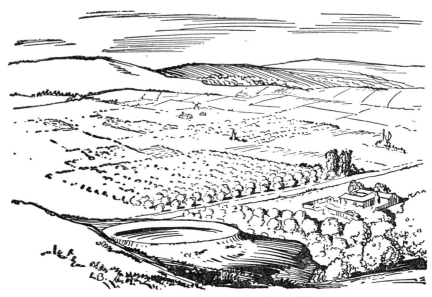

Gardens grew green in the valleys

partment of Agriculture in Washington. They were navel orange trees from Brazil—trees that have seedless fruit. The little trees grew and thrived in their new home. Buds were taken from them and grafted on small seedling trees, until many groves of trees of these fine seedless oranges were growing and bearing fruit. The navel oranges ripen from October till May. So Valencia oranges were planted to ripen in the summer months. Lemon trees were planted, and, later on, grapefruit trees.

All kinds of citrus fruits do well in southern California. Oranges were tried farther north, and they grew equally well,

186

Orange groves spread over the hillsides

ripening even earlier. Wherever water was brought to the soil, the beautiful glossy green of the orange groves spread across the California hillsides. The rich perfume of the blossoms drifted down the valleys. Golden fruit shone under green leaves.

Packing houses were built, where the fruit could be washed, sorted, and wrapped. Freight cars creaked along the siding to receive the packed boxes of fruit. In a single recent year, 150,000 carsful rolled eastward. How astonished the mission friars would have been if they could have seen long freight trains winding across the desert to carry oranges and lemons to

187

the cities of the eastern coast. This is one of the miracles water has performed in California.

Just as interesting as the story of the orange is the story of the grape. Grapes were planted in early Spanish days at all the missions. The largest vineyard belonged to San Gabriel. It was called the "mother vineyard," because it supplied the vines for so many later vineyards. Its grapes were reddish-black and very sweet. Most of the mission grapes were used for winemaking. But in mission days the grape harvest was uncertain. In dry years there were few grapes.

When the Americans came, the mission vineyards were only withered stumps in a tangle of weeds. The new citizens of California set out many different kinds of grapevines. Some came from the eastern states, some from Spain and France. Grapes would grow almost anywhere in California except on the mountains. But they flourished best in the San Joaquin and Sacramento valleys. The grapes were made into wine, or were packed and shipped as fresh fruit, or they were dried for raisins. Miles of grapevines were planted and irrigated by water brought from the mountain streams.

About the time Mrs. Tibbets was setting out her new orange trees, a man named William Thompson brought three grape cuttings to Sutter County. The cuttings were from vines on which seedless grapes grew. They had come across the sea from Constantinople. Two of the cuttings were killed in a flood. The third lived and became the parent vine of all the Thompson seedless grapes in California.

188

THE PROBLEM OF WATER

It was found that these sweet little seedless grapes and larger grapes, called "muscats," made delicious raisins when dried. In the San Joaquin valley the hot sun of summer sweetened the grapes on the vines. Then it beat down on the trays of gathered clusters, drying the juice and turning it to sugar. The little town of Fresno in the middle of the valley became the raisin center of the world. Tons of raisins from Fresno travel by train and by ship all over the world. This was another miracle of work and water in California.

In the years just after the gold rush, two Frenchmen, whose name was Pellier, had a tree nursery near the old pueblo town of San José. They went home to France and brought back prune cuttings. These they grafted on plum-tree roots. Fruit growers came to see the sturdy young prune trees and bought trees for themselves from the Pelliers. Prune orchards soon spread across the Santa Clara valley south of San Francisco Bay.

Peach, pear, plum, and apple trees were planted in sheltered valleys and on the hillsides. Fruits of all kinds grew abundantly. Walnut trees loved the California climate. Large groves were set out, and they flourished. Their thick green shade patterns the brown of the valleys in summer. Their limbs are smooth and bare in winter. Apricots and almonds, not widely or easily grown in other states, do well in California. Their blossoms fill the valleys with clouds of palest pink and white. California is like a fruit basket for the nation. All that the trees ask is unfailing water. And this the Californians have learned to provide.

The population of California grew rapidly. People came to raise fruit. They came to drill oil wells. All these people had to be fed. There was greater need for gardens. Where the two great rivers meet and flow into San Francisco Bay the land is rich with loam. Everything grows here—grows fast and large. Tilled fields stretch in a wide checker-board around the bay. There are fields of asparagus, celery, lettuce, tomatoes. More gardens were planted in the San Joaquin valley. Farms and vegetable fields spread out in a fan on the sunny lands around Los Angeles.

The strangest garden of all was made in the Imperial Valley. This valley was the burning desert which Captain Anza had crossed with his settlers from Sonora. The miracle of Imperial Valley was the result of a great idea and of the courage to see that idea carried through. Irrigation water was brought to the valley from the Colorado River, more than fifty miles away.

It took years of planning and work to accomplish this. A long canal was built to carry the water from the river to the desert valley. Disasters and delays hindered the work. When the canal was completed, the hardest blow fell. In a flood year, 1906, the river rose, broke through its new banks and covered the countryside. It had to be sent back into its course again. This took years, but it was done. At last the cruel blazing desert became the most fertile and wonderful garden spot ever known. The fierce heat which tortured travelers in the old days now ripens delicious melons and grows fine, large early vegetables for the whole United States.

As the population of California grew, the water problem grew also. It had to be worked out over and over again. The city of Los Angeles grew very fast. It was plain that the water supply would soon fall short of the needs of the citizens. Engineers were chosen to look for a new source of water.

The Owens River carried snow water from the high Sierras down into the desert on the eastern side of California. The engineers decided to bring this water two hundred and fifty miles to Los Angeles. It was a daring idea. Five thousand men worked for five years. They built pipe lines under the desert, tunnels through the mountains, bridges over deep canyons, and canals through the valleys. When these were completed, the Owens River flowed into the reservoirs of the city, a splendid water supply for the people of Los Angeles.

In 1906 an earthquake shook the whole western coast. In San Francisco the reservoirs were cracked by the strain and the water was lost. A fire which followed could not be put out. A large part of the city was burned. It was a terrible fire. Homes and business buildings were destroyed. Lives were lost.

But the people of San Francisco met this tragedy bravely. They set to work at once and rebuilt the city by the Golden Gate. The new city was a bigger and more beautiful place than the old one had been.

Steady growth followed. The time came when San Francisco needed a greater water supply. Her engineers, like those of Los Angeles, went to the high mountains to find a lasting source of water. It was found in the Hetch Hetchy Valley. This valley was in Yosemite National Park, and it could not be used without permission from the United States Government. This was gained. Then the water must be brought to San Francisco.

It was a longer and more costly work than the Owens River project. Many miles of tunnels were needed. Dams and power houses had to be built. Unexpected delays arose. But it was carried through, and San Francisco made sure of enough water for a city of five million people, if so much should ever be needed.

This is not yet the whole story of water. Two other things are tied up with this story of California's water problem— power and flood control. The dams that were built all over California do three things. First, they store water to irrigate fields and orchards and to supply the needs of people in the towns. Second, they hold back the sudden heavy rainfall which once made the streams overflow. Enough is allowed to pass through the dams to keep a normal flow in the streams, but enough is held back so that the streams do not overflow their banks and flood the countryside. Third, they furnish water power, a very important thing in a state with almost no coal.

The water that passes through the dams to the irrigation ditches turns the wheels of electric generators called "turbines." The turbines change the force of the water into power

192

called "hydroelectric power." (*Hydro* means *water*.) This power can be sent as current over electric wires for long distances. It provides lights for towns and cities. It sends trolley cars speeding along the rails. It runs elevators and factory machinery.

Because hydroelectric power was plentiful and cheap, manufacturing grew up in California. In the north, busy mills sawed the redwood forests into lumber. In the fruit and vegetable regions of the central valleys, canning factories sprang up, and factories to make farm machinery. In the south, automobile and airplane factories were built. The growth of California's industry was another result of the solving of her water problem.

One of the largest dams in the world is Boulder Dam on the Colorado River. This great dam was built by the government of the United States for California and her neighbor states of the dry Southwest. It serves the same three purposes as the smaller dams. It has tamed the raging waters of the Colorado, and ended all danger of floods in that region. It has harnessed the force of the swift current and turned it into hydroelectric power for scores of cities and towns. It has created a lasting water supply for many growing cities of southern California, and for irrigated lands. New thousands of acres of desert in Imperial Valley have been turned into garden land. And the water for this valley comes through an all-American canal. It no longer comes through the old canal which ran for many miles through Mexico.

CALIFORNIA

This is the story of water in California. It is not a finished story yet. Wise far-seeing men have studied the water needs of the state. They have found that the Sacramento Valley has much more water than is used. Every year water runs to the sea or overflows across the countryside and is wasted. This water is needed in the San Joaquin Valley, where the rivers shrink small in the heat of summer. Some day the two great rivers may be connected by a mighty canal, which will bring the extra water of the northern valley to the streams of the southern. This will add a new chapter to the story of water in California.

✞✚✦✚✦✚✦✚✦✚✦✚✦✚✦✚✦✚✦✚✦✚✦✚✦✚✦✚✦✚✦✚✦✚✦✞✞✚

CHAPTER XX

The Playground of America

IN 1914 something very important happened. It was im-
portant to the whole United States, but specially important to
California. The Panama Canal, built by the United States
Government, was completed and opened.

This canal across the Isthmus of Panama enabled large
ocean liners and all sorts of ships carrying freight to come
much more directly from the East to California ports. They
no longer need go far south around Cape Horn. Here was a
new way from the eastern to the western coast of the United
States, and a short way from California to Europe. The
dreams of the old Spanish sea captains had come true at last.
This was a glorious Strait of Anian. It was not far from the
spot where Balboa first looked out upon the Pacific Ocean.

The opening of the Panama Canal made California's commerce leap ahead. Los Angeles harbor became one of the
largest export harbors of the nation. Through the Panama
Canal the oil and fruits of California went out to half the
world. The city of Los Angeles grew in population until it

passed the million mark and became the fifth largest city of the United States.

The beautiful sheltered Bay of San Diego had its share of the new growth. San Diego harbor became the Pacific base of the United States battle fleet.

The harbor of San Francisco contains no less than fourteen ports, busy with commerce. The towns on the shores of the great bay grew into large cities. Ferry boats plied back and forth across the bay between San Francisco on the peninsula and Oakland and Berkeley on the opposite shore.

"How much better it would be," said the Californians, "if there were a bridge between these cities!"

"What?" said everyone else. "Build a bridge over five miles of water? Impossible!"

But Californians had heard the word *impossible* before. They only laughed at it. Engineers went to work on plans. Money was raised. Not one, but two great bridges were built over San Francisco Bay.

One of these bridges joins San Francisco with the city of Oakland on the eastern shore of the bay. This bridge has two decks, the upper one for six lanes of automobiles, the lower for three lanes of motor trucks and two tracks for electric trains. The bridge is in two sections. One reaches from San Francisco to the high rocky island of Yerba Buena in the center of the bay. The other reaches from Yerba Buena to Oakland. The sections are connected by a very large tunnel cut through the solid rock of the island.

196

The other bridge is a suspension bridge spanning the famous Golden Gate, at the entrance of the bay. At either side of the Gate a high tower of steel was built. Thousands of strands of heavy wire were woven back and forth between these towers. Then these wires were pressed together into solid cables. Upon these great cables was hung the Golden Gate Bridge, the largest single span in the world. It is wide enough

The Golden Gate Bridge

for six lanes of automobiles. It is high enough for the tallest ships to pass beneath. It connects San Francisco and Southern California with the Redwood Highway leading north. It is one link in the long Coast Highway from Mexico to Canada.

Suppose Lieutenant Ayala, who first entered San Francisco Bay in 1775 in the little *San Carlos,* could sail again through the Golden Gate! How he would stare! He would stand on his deck dumb with amazement at the great cities surrounding the bay, the steamships from all over the world, and the long bridges spanning the bay like miracles.

Less than two hundred years ago California was a wilderness, where only Indians dwelt. Now it is a land of civilization and culture. On the hills overlooking the bay rises the University of California, one of the greatest of all state universities. South of San Francisco, not far away, is another university, founded by one of California's pioneers, Leland Stanford. In the south the University of Southern California has grown with the growth of Los Angeles. Hundreds of colleges, schools, libraries, museums, and art centers dot the state.

Scientists watch the stars from Lick Observatory in the bay region and from the summit of Mount Wilson in the south. At California Institute of Technology in Pasadena a telescope reflector two hundred inches across is being polished. This greatest telescope of all will soon be placed on Palomar Mountain near San Diego.

The years since 1900 have made California America's largest playground. All the year round people come from the other states to spend vacation days in California. This is because her climate is comfortable and her scenery beautiful and varied. In the cruel deserts where one hundred years ago men and women and children died of hunger and thirst stand beautiful hotels. There are fountains and swimming pools, shaded courts, and restaurants with delicious foods.

In the rugged mountains, whose drifted snows barred the way of the gold seekers, are ski and toboggan slides. Here are more hotels, with warm cabins to take care of those who come for winter sports. The beaches where the Indians gathered shells to use for money are crowded with visitors. All the year round children play in the sand and brown life-guards watch swimmers in the surf.

The Government has set aside four National Parks, so that all people may have opportunity to see the natural wonders of this part of the country. Sequoia National Park is a region of mighty mountains. From Mount Whitney, the highest peak in the United States, one can look down into Death Valley, below sea level. In this park and in General Grant Park close by are the greatest of the famous Big Trees. These giant red-woods are called the world's oldest living things.

Yosemite National Park covers a thousand square miles of mountain country, full of waterfalls, rivers and lakes. Within it is the famous Yosemite Valley. Lassen National Park in the north is a land of volcanic cones and old lava beds. Here rises Mount Lassen, the only volcano in the United States which has been recently active.

One of the points of interest to visitors in southern California is the motion-picture industry. Early motion pictures were made in sunlight. Constant sunshine and varied scenery brought the motion-picture industry to Hollywood, a part of Los Angeles. They came here because land was cheap and because the weather was mild enough for outdoor work at all seasons.

These things are not so necessary now. The wonderful klieg

lights make it possible to take pictures indoors. But the studios stay in California because they are all here and because they help one another. No studio has enough of the large expensive lights for the biggest scenes. They borrow one another's lights. They borrow one another's actors and directors also. Then there are thousands of people living in the city of Los Angeles who make their living taking part in mob or crowd scenes. They are called "extras." They work a few days at a time for modest pay at any studio that needs them.

Each studio is really a little town in itself, surrounded by a high wall or fence. It contains cottages where the film stars live while working on pictures. It has great covered "daylight stages," and others where only the brilliant electric lights are used. There are costume rooms, carpenter shops, garages, machine shops and lunchrooms. There are places for the animals which take part in pictures. There are offices for writers, directors, and advertising men. The spaces between these buildings are constructed to look like the streets of many different countries. They provide scenery which can be used in films.

The studios have long ago outgrown Hollywood. The increasing need for more space forced them to locate farther from the business section. They are scattered through the northern and western suburbs of Los Angeles. This is true also of the screen actors and actresses. Some still live in Hollywood, but far more live in other sections. Because of long association, however, the world still thinks of Hollywood as the most famous center of the motion-picture industry.

200

THE PLAYGROUND OF AMERICA

It is the work of many of the people of California to make the thousands of visitors comfortable and to entertain them. Most California towns have their own fruit festival, a gay fiesta, or a historical pageant. Each old mission has its tale to tell.

Hundreds of miles of wide hard highways have been built for the motor cars which come from every state in the Union. They pass through the redwood groves of the north and the orange groves of the south. They follow the desert valleys and the mountain passes to beautiful or unusual places.

The visitors to California are interested in the rice fields of the Sacramento River, and in the acres of flowers grown for their seeds south of San Francisco. They go to see the gardens of arching date palms in the Coachella Valley, and they drive through miles of lima-bean fields along the coast near San Diego.

The motor cars stop beside ruined missions with stone arches where hung the Spanish bells. The visitors walk under gray old olive trees to look at crumbling walls and little rooms that still stand. They hear the stories of daring Spanish explorers and devoted grey-robed friars. They hear how California was held safely from other nations until the Americans came to claim her as a state. They understand that these stories belong to America's past, just as much as California with all her beauty and her plenty belongs to America's present.

The twentieth century has made great changes in the affairs of the world. Once the Atlantic Ocean was the highway of nations. The Pacific was a far and lonely sea bordered by strange and unknown lands. But now the nations of the Orient are awake. China and Japan, Australia and the South American Republics are helping to make world history. The Pacific Ocean, like the Atlantic, is a highway of commerce and travel. What was once the wilderness back yard of America has become a busy and fortunate place. And California with her three great ports has come to be another front gate through which America faces the world.

Redwood Groves of the North

Important Dates

+++

1542, September 28—Cabrillo discovered San Diego Bay.
1579, June 17—Drake landed in California, probably at Drake's Bay.
1602, December 16—Vizcaíno anchored in Monterey Bay.
1769, July 16—San Diego (first mission) founded by Junipero Serra.
1769, November 1—San Francisco Bay discovered by Jose Francisco Ortega.
1770, June 3—San Carlos (second mission) founded.
1771, July 14—San Antonio (third mission) founded.
1771, September 8—San Gabriel (fourth mission) founded.
1772, September 1—San Luis Obispo (fifth mission) founded.
1775, August 5—Ayala, in the San Carlos, entered San Francisco Bay.
1776, January 4—Anza, with his Sonora colonists, reached San Gabriel Mission.
1776, September 17—San Francisco presidio founded.
1776, October 9—San Francisco (sixth mission) founded.
1776, November 1—San Juan Capistrano (seventh mission) founded.
1777, January 12—Santa Clara (eighth mission) founded.
1777, November 29—San Jose pueblo founded.
1781, September 4—Los Angeles pueblo founded.
1782, March 31—San Buenaventura (ninth mission) founded.
1782, April 21—Santa Barbara presidio founded.
1784, August 28—death of Junipero Serra (Father President) at San Carlos.
1786, December 4—Santa Barbara (tenth mission) founded.
1787, December 8—La Purísima Concepción (eleventh mission) founded.
1791, August 28—Santa Cruz (twelfth mission) founded.
1791, October 9—Soledad (thirteenth mission) founded.
1797, June 11—San Jose (fourteenth mission) founded.
1797, June 24—San Juan Bautista (fifteenth mission) founded.
1797, July 25—San Miguel (sixteenth mission) founded.
1797, September 8—San Fernando (seventeenth mission) founded.
1798, June 13—San Luis Rey (eighteenth mission) founded.
1803, June 26—death of Father Lasuen at San Carlos.

IMPORTANT DATES

1804, September 17—Santa Ines (nineteenth mission) founded.

1817, December 14—San Rafael (twentieth mission) founded.

1822, April 11—End of Spanish rule in California, Mexican empire proclaimed.

1823, July 4—San Francisco Solano (twenty-first mission) founded.

1825, March 26—California became a territory of Mexican Republic.

1826, November 27—Jedediah Smith and trappers arrived at San Gabriel.

1843, May 1—Thomas Larkin appointed United States Consul at Monterey.

1846, June 14—Bear Flag Revolt at Sonoma.

1846, July 7—American flag raised at Monterey by order of Commodore Sloat.

1846, October 8—Battle of Dominguez Rancho.

1846, December 6—Battle of San Pasqual.

1847, January 8—Battle of San Gabriel River.

1847, January 9—Battle of Los Angeles River.

1847, January 10—Los Angeles retaken.

1847, January 13—Treaty of Cahuenga Ranch signed by Pico and Fremont.

1848, January 24—James Marshall discovered gold in the American River.

1848, February 2—Mexican War ended, Treaty gave California to United States.

1849, October 13—First constitution of California adopted at Monterey.

1850, September 9—President Fillmore signed bill admitting California to Union.

1861, October 24—transcontinental telegraph completed.

1869, May 10—Union Pacific Railroad completed.

Foreign Words and Names

✛✛✛✛✛✛✛✛✛✛✛✛✛✛✛✛✛✛✛✛✛✛✛✛✛✛✛✛✛✛✛✛✛✛✛✛✛✛

In Spanish *a* always sounds like *ah; e* always sounds like *ay; i* always sounds like *ee*. The pronunciation used here is the *Spanish American,* in which *ll* has the sound of *y* and soft *c* the sound of *s*.

Acapulco (ah-cah-pool′-co)

adobe (a-do′-bay), stiff clay, dried in the sun

Albuquerque (al-boo-ker′-ky)

Andrés (An-dres′), Andrew

Anián (An-yan′)

Antonio (An-ton′-yo), Anthony

Anza (Ahn′-sa)

atole (ah-to′-lay), gruel of maize flour; corn meal mush

Ayala (Ah-yah′-lah)

Bautista (Bow-tees′-ta), the Baptist

brea (bray′-a), pitch

Bucareli (Boo-ca-ray′-lee)

Buenaventura (Bway-na-ven-too′-ra), good fortune

Cabrillo (Ca-bree′-yo)

Cahuenga (Ca-wen′-ga)

camino (cah-mee′-no), highway

Capistrano (Cah-pees-trah′-no)

Carillo (Cah-ree′-yo)

Carlos (Car′-los), Charles

carreta (car-ray′-ta), long narrow cart

Castro (Cah′-stro)

Catalina (Cah-tah-lee′-na), Catherine

Concepción (Con-sep-syon′)

Cortés (Cor-tess′)

Crespí (Cress-pee′)

Croix (Crwah)

Cruz (Crooss), cross

de (day), of

Diego (Dee-ay′-go), James

Dolores (Do-lo′-ress), sorrows

Domínguez (Do-meen′-guess)

el, the

Española (Es-pan-yo′-la), Spanish

Estevan (Es-tay′-van), Steven

Fages (Fah′-hess)

Farallones (Fah-rah-yo′-ness)

Felipe (Fay-lee′-pay), Philip

Fernando (Fer-nan′-do), Ferdinand

Ferrelo (Fer-ray′-lo)

fiesta (fee-es′-ta), merrymaking

Figueroa (Fee-gay-ro′-a)

Flores (Flo′-ress)

Francisco (Fran-sees′-co), Francis

Gabriel (Gah-bree-ale′)

Galvez (Gal′-vess)

Gaspar (Gah-spar′)

gavilán (gah-vee-lahn′), sparrowhawk

Hernando (Er-nan′-do)

Inés (Ee-ness′), Inez

José (Ho-say′), Joseph

Juan (Hwan), John

Junípero (Hoo-nee′-pay-ro), juniper

205

Kino (Kee'-no)
la, the
las, the
Lasuén (Lah-swain')
los, the
Luis (Lweess), Louis
Majorca (Ma-hor'-ca), an island near the coast of Spain
mantilla (man-tee'-ya), a lace mantle for the hair
Margarita (Mar-gah-ree'-ta)
María (Mah-ree'-a), Mary
Mendoza (Men-do'-sa)
Miguel (Mee-gale')
Misión (Mee-syon'), Mission
Mojave (Mo-hah'-vay), an Indian tribe
Monterey (Mon-ter-ay')
Montezuma (Mon-tay-su'-ma)
Moraga (Mo-rah'-ga)
Navidad (Nah-vi-dad')
Neve (Nay'-vay)
nuestra (nwes'-tra), our
Obispo (O-bees'-po), the bishop
olla (oy'-ah), earthen jar
Ortega (Or-tay'-ga)
Palou (Pah'-loo)
panocha (pah-no'-cha), dark brown unrefined sugar
patio (pah-tyo)
Pedro (Pay'-dro), Peter
Pellier (Pel-yay')
Pérez (Per'-ess)
Pétra (Pay'-tra)
Pico (Pee'-co)
Pio (Pee'-o)
Porciúncula (Por-syoon'-coo-la), little portion, a place in Italy
pinole (pee-no'-lay), flour of roasted maize

206

pozole (po-so'-lay), a stew of corn and vegetables
Portolá (Por-to-lah')
presidio (pray-see'-dyo), fort
pueblo (poo-ay'-blo), town
Purísima (poo-ree'-see-ma), most holy
Rafael (Rah-fah-ale')
rancho (rahn'-cho), ranch
ranchería (rahn-chay-ree'-a), village
ranchero (rahn-chay'-ro), rancher
real (ray-ahl'), royal
Rey (ray), the king
Reyes (Ray'-ess), kings
Rivera (Ree-vay'-ra)
rodeo (ro-day'-o), round-up
Rodriguez (Ro-dree'-guess), Roderick
Salinas (Sah-lee'-nas)
San ⎱ (Sahn)
Santa ⎰ (Sahn'-ta), Saint, or holy
Santo ⎰ (Sahn'-to)
Sebastián (Say-bas-tyan')
señor (sain-yor'), Mr.
señora (sain-yo'-ra), Mrs.
Serra (Ser'-ra)
Soledad (Sol-ay-dad'), solitude
Sonoma (So-no'-ma)
Sonora (So-no'-ra)
Tehuantepec (Tay-wahn-tay-pec')
Tomás (To-mas'), Thomas
Tres (trace), three
Ulloa (oo-yo'-a)
Valencia (Vah-lain'-sya)
vaquero (vah-kay'-ro), cowboy
Vallejo (Vah-yay'-ho)
Vila (Vee'-la)
visitador (vee-see-tah'-dor)
Vizcaíno (Vees-cah-ee'-no)
Yang-Na (Yang-Na')

Index

207

INDEX

209

INDEX

INDEX